THE LIBRARY
CATALOGUE
AS SOCIAL SPACE

THE LIBRARY CATALOGUE AS SOCIAL SPACE

Promoting Patron Driven Collections, Online Communities, and Enhanced Reference and Readers' Services

Laurel Tarulli

LIBRARIES UNLIMITED

AN IMPRINT OF ABC-CLIO, LLC
Santa Barbara, California • Denver, Colorado • Oxford, England

Library of Congress Cataloging-in-Publication Data

Tarulli, Laurel.
    The library catalogue as social space : promoting patron driven collections, online communities, and enhanced reference and readers' services / Laurel Tarulli.
        p. cm.
    Includes bibliographical references and index.
    ISBN 978–1–59884–629–4 (pbk.) — ISBN 978–1–59884–630–0 (ebook) (print)
1. Online library catalogs—Technological innovations. 2. Library catalogs and users. 3. Patron–driven acquisitions (Libraries) I. Title.
Z699.35.C38T37   2012
025.3′132—dc23   2011043490

ISBN: 978–1–59884–629–4
EISBN: 978–1–59884–630–0

16 15 14 13 12   1 2 3 4 5

This book is also available on the World Wide Web as an eBook.
Visit www.abc-clio.com for details.

Libraries Unlimited
An Imprint of ABC-CLIO, LLC

ABC-CLIO, LLC
130 Cremona Drive, P.O. Box 1911
Santa Barbara, California 93116-1911

This book is printed on acid-free paper ∞

Manufactured in the United States of America

For my husband Franco, daughter Amelia, and Mom and Dad.

CONTENTS

FOREWORD

The way we look at library catalogues is changing. They are no longer just the linear lists of book or card catalogues or the extension of those lists in our current online catalogues. They are not just the description of what we have locally but can be connected to the entire world of information. With future systems based on the conceptual model of the *Functional Requirements for Bibliographic Records* (FRBR), we can take the perspective of the broader bibliographic universe with all the relationships and interconnections that will help our users find things they want.

We can build on a basic bibliographic description from authors and publishers, augmented by the skills of our technical services staff. That identifying data can be further augmented with summaries or abstracts, suggestions, recommendations, additional names, subjects, and other data from our pubic services staff and users or other third-party sources available on the Web—information our users want.

In addition, the Internet has opened up new technological capabilities that enable libraries to be a key part of the larger information community. We are no longer restricted to providing our services when our buildings are open. For the materials that are digital or have been digitized, we are no longer restricted to providing our collections only at the hours when our buildings are open. We can offer our services and collections to everyone in the world at whatever time they want to find something. With future systems (and some current ones), we can connect our users to "more like this" and "if you liked this, you might like ..." —based on capabilities we've seen on the Web, using data directly provided by other users or staff or computed through circulation data.

This is an amazing time of transition from old views of catalogues to new opportunities. This book describes many such opportunities, especially for collaborative efforts to improve user services. Embrace the change and join others to make things better!

Barbara B. Tillett, Ph.D.
Chief of the Policy and Standards Division (PSD)
Library of Congress

INTRODUCTION

Why do we have a library catalogue? Do we have to alter how we view the library catalogue and its role in public libraries? If we continue to use library catalogues in public libraries, do they have to change? While the continued importance and progression of the library website from a static bulletin board to an interactive and dynamic gateway to all of the library's information is being met, addressed, and accepted with eagerness and excitement, the evolution of a library catalogue from an online version of the card catalogue into an interactive, community-driven tool has not been met with the same acceptance and enthusiasm. Understanding why the library catalogue continues to be seen as an inventory list with the majority of "wow" factors being found on the library website needs to be explored. Does it have to do with fears and traditional biases, or is it just that we haven't considered alternate or additional roles that the library catalogue can play in our library services?

Imagine being a mom-to-be nearing your due date. You want to go to the library to get some interesting books and resources on motherhood, but you're home on bed rest. What resources are available? What are the best books to read and invest in? In most cases, women turn to other women—mothers and moms-to-be for advice on books and resources. Now, imagine logging in to your local library catalogue and being able to chat with other moms, reading reviews on books written by other local mothers, and finding recommended resources that are in your neighborhood for after the baby is born. Wouldn't that be great? Can you think of numerous other scenarios where it would be an asset to read what other local community members are saying about certain books and topics: recommendations and so on?

This book provides an exploration of how and why library catalogues should and can become this online social space and community platform. In essence, it introduces ideas and provides support for library catalogues becoming an extension of our physical library's social space.

In addition to exploring the library catalogue as a social space and community platform outside the walls of our physical library, this book also explores the existing and future potential of the library catalogue and possibilities for how it can be used to enhance core library services, such as readers' services, collection development, youth services, and reference. In addition, it seeks to understand the divide between frontline staff and backroom staff and how, if increased collaboration takes place, the library catalogue can grow into a tool that benefits the entire library community as a social and dynamic space that provides local information, discovery, and resources while providing a direct link to individuals within our own communities. While examining the divide between frontline and backroom staff, differing opinions within the backroom (cataloguers) is also addressed, as are attempts to provide solutions and an understanding of the diverse opinions and ideas professionals have regarding social catalogues.

While the content of this book focuses on the library catalogue, the concepts and ideas found throughout this book are targeted toward a wider audience than just that of cataloguers and technical services staff. The library catalogue isn't just the concern of a cataloguer or your information technology (IT) department. Shaping the future of the remote public library and understanding how well positioned our catalogues are in playing a role in that future is the concern of all library professionals.

There are several terms and phrases that may be used interchangeably throughout this book. The concept of a social catalogue and next generation catalogue will be heavily used and is defined here as a new type of catalogue that has emerged out of the growing popularity of social technology. In a general sense, next generation catalogues are defined as and considered a new type or new generation of library catalogues that are emerging as the newest iteration of catalogues that incorporate technology not found in our existing "legacy" catalogues. Next generation catalogues may include social features, intuitive interfaces, faceted navigation, or any number of new technologies that did not exist in our text-based, classic (legacy) catalogues. A social catalogue implies the social nature of what a next generation catalogue is or has the potential to be. It is meant to describe a library catalogue that promotes collaboration and the invitation to generate information by users for inclusion within the catalogue. Social catalogues include features that allow for sharing data from bibliographic records with additional social networks such as Facebook, sending information through email, or saving data outside of the catalogue through social bookmarking sites. These terms are used interchangeably throughout this book.

A central theme that will be found throughout this text is the need for increased collaboration between frontline and backroom staff. This stems from the need to acknowledge that professionals' roles within the public library no longer operate in silos where one professional is an expert in only reference, only cataloguing, or only adult services. Rather, new technology has demanded that many professionals become aware of the needs in many departments. We're seeing cataloguers emerge as remote readers' advisors and frontline readers' advisors exploring the possibility of creating new subject headings that reflect current reading trends. However, without working together and understanding the nuances of each service, neither cataloguers nor readers' advisors can implement these ideas successfully when working in isolation of each other. The ability to work together and share this knowledge promotes increased access within our catalogues, successful discovery experiences among users, and an increase in the quality of services we offer users—whether they access our services remotely or from within the walls of the physical library.

I've written this book for a variety of reasons. It is meant to assist in educating library professionals; including management, about social catalogues and the impact they will have or can potentially have on staff, work flow, library services, users, and the public's perception of libraries of the future. It is also a resource that we can turn to in addressing the arguments for and against implementing social catalogues, ideas for staff buy-in, promotional opportunities, and providing concrete collaborative ideas and projects, some of which are currently being practiced in public libraries. As a result, this is not simply another publication for cataloguers and cataloguing, but a text that bridges the divide, with application to all areas of the profession seeking to implement new technologies and a social aspect to remote services and our increasing online community. Whether you're a supporter of social technology and next generation cataloguers, a naysayer, or undecided, the content presented throughout this book is of value to you.

Library 2.0 and web 2.0 caught the library profession by surprise. Rather than being on the forefront of these emerging technologies and ideas, we are struggling to catch up. While we're still focussing on the 2.0 phenomenon, our competitors, such as online bookstores, the Internet, and Google, are already seeking new ways to push web 2.0 into web 3.0 or even into a semantic web. However, rather than shrug our shoulders at missed opportunities, we're seeing an increasing number of libraries invest in social technology and promote innovative ways of using technology to encourage the sharing of information.

In public libraries, our e-branch staff are struggling to push our websites into socially interactive, online spaces that are not only inviting and easy to use but also useful. That is to say, serving a purpose and addressing users expectations, information needs and wants. While our webmasters are busily trying to integrate social tools on our web pages, readers' services staff are creating blogs to share with readers, and reference departments are developing wikis to house their resources. Many libraries are even exploring or are already offering mobile options as an additional platform for accessing library services. All of these projects and efforts are pushing libraries forward into an environment that allows us to share information and ideas not only with each other but also with our patrons. More than that, however, we're trying to seek new ways to invite patrons to provide us with information.

Libraries are inviting users to be the contributors of information. Users are not only assisting in generating the information we collect but also influencing our decisions in every area of the services we provide. This is a shift from the traditional model of libraries, as we invite patrons to assist in collection development, build and offer opinions on book lists, and influence programming. Readers' advisory services blogs, common to many public libraries, offer a good example of this invitation to collaborate with our users. Every time a readers' advisor writes a book review or presents a reading list on a library's blog, we are inviting readers to share their ideas and opinions. We are even encouraging readers to disagree with us or provide additional reading ideas that we might not have considered relevant or appropriate.

With this shift toward collaboration and community interaction, it is interesting to note that, until recently, very little 2.0 technology was starting to make its way into library catalogues. While websites change to accommodate the needs of users and readers' advisors are creating blogs to reach our readers, why isn't the catalogue taking advantage of these technologies? As the primary access tool to our libraries' collection, the library catalogue is the only face of the library many remote patrons ever see. And if this is true, then it is important to focus on the potential our library catalogues have in this new 2.0, 3.0 or even semantic technology world.

There are several ideas that need to be explored within the chapters of this book. First, there is the concept that we are inviting our users to contribute and generate information in our libraries, a responsibility that, until now, has been left only to library professionals. Then we must turn our attention to examining the ideas that the library catalogue is the new "frontline" face of the library and our main point of contact with users in this digital environment. Why is it important for our profession to reflect on what a library catalogue is? One of the most controversial topics on listservs is the definition of a catalogue and its role in the library. Should we even use the term "catalogue," or should we be seeking an alternate name and definition?

THE LIBRARY CATALOGUE

The catalogue has always been the same, reliable tool that first appeared in print form in 1595 at the Leiden University Library. However, libraries began using catalogues as early as the 800s, organizing books from their collection into categories and genres.

Today, the library catalogue bears no resemblance to those early catalogues. Or does it? Library catalogues continue to organize and categorize a library's collection. From the advent of library catalogues in the 800s to the online catalogues we use today, they have remained the primary access point to our collections. That they have improved, changed, grown, and advanced with technology cannot be argued. That our methods for organizing, classifying, and providing easier access cannot be denied.

Despite the advancements in the organization, classification, and description within library catalogues, the role of the library catalogue has largely remained the same, until recently.

With the advent of automated library catalogues, or legacy catalogues, libraries began viewing the catalogue as a different kind of tool. This transition at first appears to have happened slowly, but when recognizing that many automated library catalogues were implemented only 10 to 20 years ago in some libraries, it has actually been a speedy transition. Initially, we just entered the information found on the index cards within the card catalogue. Soon, we began adding additional content, including additional subject headings or summaries. And recently, we began adding additional language information, detailed fiction records, and even localized enriched content we believe holds value for our users.

Today, the catalogue is no longer merely an inventory to assist patrons in finding a book within the library's collection; the catalogue assists in building reading lists and determining what areas of the collection need to be developed. With the limited but useful functions that legacy catalogues are already providing, it's easy to see how next generation catalogues, with their rich features, can expand the uses and functions of this power tool. As a result, while it's true that many of the ideas and thoughts that are presented in this text are possible to implement within your own catalogues or in current next generation catalogues, some of the ideas presented have yet to become a reality, but are, instead, presented as possibilities of what is to come or what will be a reality in a few short years.

Chapter 1 examines next generation catalogues as a tool that will have a significant impact on the future of core library services. Rather than the common view that the catalogue is an inventory, this chapter explores the idea that the library catalogue can become a social space and an online community. This idea is based on including essential elements into catalogues that are already found in our physical library spaces. These elements include people, community, information, socializing, learning, and trust. While a change or expansion of the definition of a catalogue may be difficult to accept or perhaps even controversial among some professionals, reasons for why we need to explore these options and a preliminary view of the benefits must be considered. These discussions are combined with the idea that many frontline staff view the implementation of next generation catalogues as a cosmetic enhancement rather than a significant tool for change and benefit to all the services offered by the physical library.

While Chapter 1 sets out to explain how the catalogue can become an important tool to core library services, it also acknowledges its past shortcomings. These shortcomings have prevented past attempts to increase the role of the catalogue and have resulted in neglecting the important role the catalogue is positioned to take and why the library website is currently playing a role that may be a more natural fit for the library catalogue.

Chapter 2 examines what next generation catalogues, or social catalogues, are and the features they exhibit. This starts with the implementation of the first social catalogue at the University of North Carolina, where many librarians and cataloguers realized, for the first time, just what an interactive library catalogue could be when incorporating an intuitive and interactive interface. The chapter also presents a list of existing features found in social catalogues today as well as features that may be offered shortly. Definitions and explanations of some of the key elements, as well as some guidelines to assist your library in deciding what type of next generation catalogue is right for your users, are also presented.

With the emergence of next generation catalogues, professionals have developed strong opinions for and against their purposes and implementation. Even among cataloguers, there are fears regarding the integrity of our bibliographic data and the demise of our standard subject headings. However, frontline staff are also concerned about their implementation. Without a proper understanding of its features and how they work, professionals jump to erroneous conclusions about the impact these catalogues will have on their jobs. It's important to acknowledge that the fear and concern many professionals have is legitimate, especially if they are not well versed in how next generation catalogues function. Chapter 3 provides examples of common concerns regarding social catalogues that many staff have and attempts to answer these concerns logically and respectfully. One of the significant concepts of this chapter is set out by a quote from a colleague's email wherein he stated, "I seem to detect in this conversation a divide between those who live on the Net and can see its possibilities, and those who may read extensively about and even dabbled in the Net but don't live there."

After exploring the fears and excitement associated with changes in the traditional models, Chapter 4 examines the natural fit between readers' services and next generation catalogues. Understanding that readers' services is also in a transition period and steadily gaining ground as a core library service, the library catalogue is offered as a solution to many of our remote readers' needs. The catalogue, with its ability to reach shy or reluctant readers, encourages interaction among other patrons within the community and allows in-house readers' advisory experts to take advantage of a tool that will reach out to readers in their homes while travelling or any-where else they choose to be. Taking advantage of such a tool also allows readers' advisors to focus on more programs and ideas within the walls of the library, allowing the catalogue and cataloguers to assist in supporting remote access to these services. Duncan Smith, NoveList product manager for the popular readers' advisory tool NoveList, has contributed to this chapter as well. Duncan's perspective is unique because he views social cata-logues from a readers' advisory perspective rather than a cataloguing per-spective. Because this book is intended as more than just a cataloguer's resource, Duncan provides a glimpse into how vendors and frontline staff can view the implementation and potential benefits of these catalogues based on evidence gleaned from his experience and those of several libraries he has worked with closely.

While the previous chapter focuses on readers' services and the library catalogue, Chapter 5 seeks to examine the possibilities for collaboration between frontline and backroom staff in other service areas, in particular, how and why social catalogues can support and enhance our traditional library services. Ideas are presented that assist in bridging the gap between these services as the "how" behind next generation catalogues is applied to describe some of the benefits core library services will receive from these catalogues. This includes an exploration of the complementing skills library staff have and includes different perspectives and experiences that are needed when deciding on collaborative work. The examples provided within this chapter build a concrete foundation of knowledge for profes-sionals to apply within their own libraries when it comes to such things as promoting hidden library collections, promoting programs, or developing remote readers' services.

Ultimately, this chapter attempts to represent many of you, as readers, and your hesitations, excitement, or overall differing perspectives so that the con-tent provided herein can become applicable to your own positions. While it is easy to offer one perspective on the future of the library catalogue, it is always informative and interesting to examine what other professionals throughout the library industry are thinking. Duncan's essay in Chapter 4 is included to offer a different perspective than just that of a cataloguer as an expert in read-ers' services. However, Chapter 7 also offers two additional essays from lead-ers in the field. This will be discussed later in this introduction.

This book has not been written as a marketing strategy to persuade libra-ries to purchase social catalogues but rather has an intended purpose of exposing the library profession to the future functions and possibilities of library catalogues and the need for all staff throughout the library to work together. However, it needs to be acknowledged that if the concepts and ideas do persuade you that your library needs to purchase and implement a next generation catalogue, it is a reality that many libraries just aren't in a position to do so. Limited resources, resistance from management, or any number of factors play a role in whether libraries are able to acquire a social catalogue. Chapter 6 seeks to provide alternate solutions to make your existing legacy catalogue a "social" catalogue. While legacy catalogues can't provide the same features as true social catalogues, they can, with some creativity, offer some interesting and innovative ideas that enhance your library services. This chapter, more than any other, may be the most useful resource to many professionals who want to experiment with social features without committing fully to the significant investment of implementing a next generation catalogue.

The final chapter of this book, Chapter 7, explores the future of library catalogues. When this book was first started, the use of smartphones for accessing information had only begun. At the time of this reading and because of the explosive popularity and adoption of this technology, likely some of the ideas presented even in this chapter are outdated. As mobile devices make up one of the most quickly adopted technologies in history, Chapter 7 seeks to explore how these devices will play a role in the development of next generation catalogues and the features that will become important based on smartphone user's needs and wants.

Chapter 7 also examines what professionals are predicting as essential components that need to be developed to enhance existing next generation catalogues, including a more robust back end to social catalogues for the convenience of staff as well as the ability to break apart data that allow for the sharing and manipulating of only portions of bibliographic data outside of the catalogue.

Chapter 7 offers perspectives from two practicing professionals in various areas of the library profession. Brian Briscoe, the catalogue manager at St. Charles City-County Library District in St. Peters, Missouri, explores his vision of the future of the library catalogue and the direction our library catalogues need to take. Written from a cataloguing perspective, this essay shares many of the same visions other cataloguers have, acknowledging considerations that need to be made to truly achieve a next generation catalogue and possible implications for cataloguers if we abolish long-standing cataloguing practices to achieve short-term results.

Dr. Louise Spiteri, director of the School of Information Management at Dalhousie University in Halifax, Nova Scotia, offers a unique and academic perspective. Louise's essay focuses on the impact of social catalogues on cataloguing ethics. With the idea that it is an important ethical principle of cataloguing to focus on users and meeting their needs, it is also essential to consider how our cataloguing practices will be impacted in an effort to create catalogues that consider user convenience as the primary goal. This is especially true in an environment where we are attempting to meet the culturally diverse needs of a variety of communities.

Even with the opinions and ongoing discussions between leading professionals, it is hard to offer proof that these catalogues are what libraries really need or even that we are heading in the right direction. Research also plays a vital role in the future of social catalogues. This chapter examines the lack of evidence-based research on next generation catalogues and the variety of areas that currently need examining. Research, both in the academic circles and in public libraries, will provide a benchmark for future growth and development. Such evidence will, ultimately, impact how vendors view and develop library catalogues in the future. Research also provides information for public libraries to rely on when making the decision to purchase a next generation catalogue. As a result, Chapter 7 seeks to predict what we may see in the future as key elements to next generation catalogues, advancements that still need to be made, and an acknowledgment that there are key areas of these catalogues that need to be examined to ensure future growth, benefits, and potential for all library users and our library services.

Finally, ideas on marketing will be explored. While many of us are used to marketing through traditional venues such as television and radio advertisements, posters, or bookmarks, launching a social catalogue demands that we tap into social media. This goes back to the common phrase we often hear repeatedly: "You need to be where your users are." But we also need to be where are nonusers are. After all, many of these new features aren't only for our existing users but also for the groups of information-savvy nonusers who don't realize what the library can offer.

CONCLUSION

Throughout the text of this book, I've attempted to keep the tone light but the content rich with ideas and concepts on the future of the library catalogue. In particular, there is an emphasis on the library catalogue as a social space and online community in an attempt to explore how and why the library catalogue is an essential element in the continued success of library services and the expectations that patrons have with respect to the remote delivery of these services. Also important and complementing the light tone is the attempt to stay positive and point out the merits of social catalogues. While some readers may find the position too one sided and optimistic, the purpose of this book is to bring forward positive and exciting projects and potential in our library catalogues and the benefits of working together with patrons and with other professionals.

Although written by a librarian and cataloguer, the content found throughout this book is applicable to professionals who work throughout the many areas of services within a public library. In particular, it is hoped that the material is presented in a way that will encourage frontline and backroom staff to explore the possibilities of working together and to spark innovative and creative ideas in all library services when it comes to the library catalogue and the rich and strong potential it poses for delivering information in a socially engaged and interactive environment.

CHAPTER 1

The Library Catalogue as a Social Space

The library catalogue is no longer an inventory but a place, and an online community. All that we have come to believe about the function of the catalogue and the role of the library catalogue in libraries is challenged by taking the position that the library catalogue is more than an inventory of a library's collection but is also a social space and an online community. This concept forces the profession to rethink how we use the catalogue, moving away from a database that assists in accessing a library's collection to a space that not only provides access but also encourages patron and staff interaction, aids in collection development, enhances readers' services, and, overall, impacts every level of library service within the physical branch as well as remotely. If we accept that the library catalogue is also a social, collaborative space, we are redefining the meaning of the library catalogue and, as a result, the role of the library catalogue in all aspects of library services. And if the library catalogue is more than just an inventory but also an interactive, social portal that leads to discovery and interaction, what does this mean to you as a library administrator? A librarian? A readers' advisor?

There is a significant amount of skepticism that accompanies the enhancement of a tool that has the potential to impact every aspect of library service. How can a library catalogue be an online community without being a social network? If the library catalogue becomes the primary destination spot for our remote users, what happens to our library website? What happens to the physical branch and the roles we've traditionally defined ourselves by? If a library catalogue is a social space, the definition of an e-branch and the focus of the library Web page as the central hub of that electronic branch is also challenged.

Despite the many questions professionals have, even those viewing these new catalogues with skepticism can't deny the excitement and the enticing potential of the roles and impact that social catalogues may have on the profession. To be sure, a fair amount of skepticism and concern are reasonable reactions when we consider the impact they will have on all of us and the lack of literature and research that exists on social catalogues and their features and use in libraries. However, this book is based on the premise that the library catalogue is a social space that promotes community. And not only is this true, but the changing role of the library catalogue is occurring right now. It is up to us as a profession, however, to decide how or if we will take advantage of the opportunity this presents to us as well as how we will react to this change.

Take, for instance, the traditional role of a readers' advisor. Readers' advisors (RAs) play a vital role in today's public libraries. Taking library services to its most personal level, they engage readers in conversation that assist them in making reading suggestions in an effort to find readers "that perfect book." Generating reading lists based on their professional expertise and training that draw together books based on factors like read-alikes, appeals, or genres are a vital part of what an RA does today. But what if the library catalogue could do that? What if cataloguers started playing a role in the creation of lists based on patron recommendations, reader generated book lists, or reviews? What would remain of the role of readers' advisor?

Although this scenario will be explored later in this book, your minds can rest at ease. While next generation catalogues, or social catalogues, have every possibility of fulfilling the scenario just described, they will in no way diminish the need for frontline readers' advisors. However, they will change the traditional role of RAs, enhancing this service and allowing staff members to explore and take advantage of opportunities that haven't been available to them in the past. What is important is that readers' advisors understand how social catalogues will complement RA services rather than diminish the role of RAs. But preparation and understanding is essential for taking advantage of such a powerful tool.

Not fully understanding what next generation catalogues are and how they can impact library services as well as the day-to-day staff activities in the library leads to skepticism, distrust, and fear. This is a natural reaction to change, especially significant change to what has been a very traditional, clearly defined tool.

Almost as controversial as doing away with the Dewey decimal classification system, cataloguers are, perhaps, more divided in their opinions on next generation library catalogues and their role in libraries than any other professional. These new social catalogues will impact cataloguing practices, requiring new skills, increasing demands on cataloguing, impacting cataloguing practices, and shedding light on the backroom mystique surrounding the library catalogue and cataloguing. Of considerable concern is the impact on the integrity of the metadata found in the catalogue, redefining the catalogue out of existence, or adding so much content that it will be impossible to manage. Also the cause of much debate is the additional user-generated information included in bibliographic records that presents the possibility, among other things, of influencing a catalogue's controlled vocabulary. This is all compounded by concerns over the additional role that cataloguers will now have to play, as social catalogues will provide a platform to increase backroom staff and frontline staff collaboration and interaction.

Social catalogues provide a concrete and very strong bond that will finally assist in bridging the gap and putting an end to the lack of collaboration and communication that has traditionally been found among frontline and backroom staff in public libraries. No longer will frontline staff only interact with cataloguers when there are misspellings in the catalogue, errors in call numbers, or missing genre stickers. Cataloguers will become frontline staff and vice versa. While the hands-on responsibilities will remain largely the same, social catalogues will allow both sides of the profession a greater glimpse into how our roles impact and complement each other and, with luck, diminish some of the frustration we often feel with each other and various practices within the library due to misunderstandings.

This brings us back to asking the question, what is a library catalogue, and why, or perhaps how, can the catalogue be a social space or a community?

Emerging social technologies and intuitive software has all of us asking why we still use library catalogues and, more important, why our catalogues are so difficult to use. Google, Amazon, LibraryThing, and Facebook have all changed the way we view our online environment and the ever-expanding possibilities that environment offers. Most of us belong to some sort of social network, have several email accounts, and habitually use Wikipedia, Google, or Amazon to answer our questions. In fact, even as librarians, we are likely to use online resources to answer questions in our personal and professional lives before using the library catalogue. For example, readers' advisors are the first to admit they use the database NoveList or the Genreflecting book series to find read-alikes rather than using the library catalogue. And users routinely search Google for information before using the library or Amazon for book recommendations before returning to the library catalogue to place their hold. While library catalogues and libraries used to be the primary source of information for our users, today, we are not even competitors among the many sources that do it better than us, with an ease and purpose that we have not yet been able to achieve considering the expectations of today's users. And yet, when we look at social networking sites, collaborative sites, and successful online environments, we see a combination of what the library is all about: people, community, information, socializing, learning, and trust.

The library, now more than ever, has become a social gathering place for our community. This is never so apparent than when community members who aren't library patrons book our rooms for events and meetings or teenagers drop in after school to chat, text their friends, or listen to their iPods. The physical library is a popular gathering place because it is centrally located and convenient. Libraries are easy to access and provide immediate gratification of users' needs—even if it isn't what the user expected or wanted. Does this sound familiar? The physical library is and continues to be successful because it provides the same type of elements that the Internet provides—convenience, ease of use, location, social interaction, and information. But the one thing the physical library can't do is be where the people are—in homes, on the bus, at the airport, or at the grocery store. However, library websites and, more specifically, library catalogues can.

While the Web 2.0 movement has caused the entire library profession to review core services, it has caused a large wake-up call to integrated library system (ILS) vendors, cataloguers, and software developers. As early as 1987, the cataloguing community was talking about library catalogues that could rank results by relevancy, seek user feedback, provide faceted navigation, and search natural language vocabularies. With the emergence of the 2.0 movement, the theories and ideas that had been suggested and talked about for 20 years became a reality. Unfortunately, that reality was realized through the online environment rather than through library catalogues.

Until recently, library catalogues have always been inventory-based electronic versions of the card catalogue. The catalogue's sole purpose has been and continues to be to provide access to a library's collection. Unfortunately, this has not always been successful because of the limitations presented by online public access catalogues (OPACs). While the accuracy and quality of content can't be argued, the usefulness of the library catalogue in an age of interaction, discovery, and immediacy is being questioned. Is there a future for the library catalogue? What will tomorrow's catalogues look like? Should we migrate all of our information to our website?

It was only after North Carolina State University Libraries implemented Endeca in 2006 that the true potential of library catalogues became realized. Endeca is more of a search engine than a catalogue interface, giving users more of a Google search experience than a database searching experience. However, with its feature-rich capabilities, first realized on commercial sites such as Barnes & Noble and Home Depot, the possibilities of combining such a product with the rich metadata found in bibliographic records began finding its way into academic libraries and professional literature. Endeca made it possible for the library community and particularly the cataloguing community to realize not only that there is a future for library catalogues but also that the future will impact the entire profession. This includes core library services that have, up until now, functioned in relative isolation from library catalogues. While Endeca was one of the first and most well known examples of the social catalogue, vendors are busy creating their own versions of these catalogues, as are open-source software developers. Unfortunately, few professionals outside of the cataloguing community are still aware of the possibilities these catalogues hold for enhancing the entire library experience.

THE LIBRARY CATALOGUE IS A GATHERING PLACE AND A COMMUNITY

Like a mantra that we use to live by, it is important to repeat once again that the library catalogue is no longer just an inventory but also a gathering place and a community. Public library catalogues exist to provide access to collections for their users. These users tend to be local, location-specific users with identified information needs and cultural identities. Unlike the Internet as a whole, the library catalogue seeks to serve a select group of individuals, attempting to target their needs and wants while reflecting their cultural differences and languages. A colleague once expressed his view of the ideal library catalogue as a "localized Google." And, with the development of these new, next generation catalogues, it can be—but even better. The library catalogue has an advantage over other online information resources; it's an extension of a physical environment where relationships and a level of trust with the community already exists.

And, while we are now accustomed to defining our branches as social spaces, we are still based on the premise that patrons use our library primarily to access our collections. If we still believe that our collections are important—and perhaps the most important part of our library—then we also need to seriously explore the idea of the library catalogue as a collaborative and interactive space. It provides not only the social features sought by many of our community members but also access to all of our collections, many of which are now online. In fact, social catalogues provide the branch library experience virtually. They can link to recorded author readings or programs and provide pathways to program announcements, special events within the library, and links into the greater community.

Isn't that the role of the library website? Don't we have enough online communities? Why muddy the waters by throwing the library catalogue into the mix? Social catalogues, however, aren't like a Second Life virtual community or a social networking site such as Facebook. This new generation of library catalogues seeks to bring like-minded patrons together, encourage the sharing of information, invite community-created information, and act not only as a place of discovery for the local library collection but also as a gateway to information far beyond the walls of the library. But these catalogues aren't just about fostering a community among our patrons; they are a way to develop and extend relationships of trust and community between our staff and patrons remotely—patrons who may never walk through the doors of the physical library.

While libraries offer programs, meeting room spaces, literacy classes, and a variety of other activity-related events, the library is still viewed as a place to check out books, DVD, CDs, and other materials. It is the local destination to find out of print books, access old newspaper articles, or check resources that either require subscriptions or can't be obtained by individuals. At its core, the library is still very much about its collection—electronic, downloadable, or physical. It is with this in mind that we have to look at the library catalogue. If a public library's collection is central to the purpose, perhaps even the existence of the library, then doesn't it mean that the library catalogue must be considered an integral tool? The library catalogue is the public library's central tool and face of the library. It is the new "front line" of the library. Unfortunately, because of the traditional restrictions of library catalogues and its technology, the website—a tool far newer than the library catalogue—has surpassed the catalogue in priority and role within our libraries.

The library catalogue has the potential to be the central destination spot for the library's e-branch or online environment. Why the catalogue and not the website? In the past, the website has been the primary, frontline face of the library because traditional online catalogues did not have the ability to sustain anything greater than that of a supporting role. An inability to customize and add links as well as the difficulty in upgrading to new versions provided a rigid structure that made the website an attractive and easy alternative. However, today's catalogues can provide an intuitive, customizable interface that can be a gateway into the library's website as well as the numerous resources and collections in the library's holdings. Most notable is that the real promise of creating the catalogue as the library's primary destination spot is the focus on user personalization, customization, access, and sharing.

To be a community space, the library catalogue does not have to become another social networking site. Users already belong to social networking sites. This is something that many professionals question when they hear that the library catalogue can become a social space and an online community. Library patrons who visit the physical library branch belong to the culture and community within that branch or library system. The sense of community they share in this social space has to do with trust, familiar faces, comfortable surroundings, and the knowledge that they are in a safe, communal environment. A patron knows that it is acceptable to walk up to another patron to comment on a book, a DVD, or a program. He also knows that as much as he loves the latest Linwood Barclay thriller, there are hundreds of other local community members who do also because of the amount of holds on the items and the wear and tear of his library's copy.

It is with these examples in mind that we can grow the library catalogue into an online, social space.

Rather than thinking of the library catalogue as an inventory or a static database or even a social networking site where everyone has to participate, the library catalogue should be considered as an online, virtual experience of walking through the library's stacks. You see "Steve" in the mystery section because that's the only thing he reads. And there's "Amelia," the woman who is determined to read every new romance and then critique it as well as any *New York Times* reviewer. And, of course, there's "Sue," who never says anything, but you can always tell she's listening to other patrons talk about books and watching what is on the staff's newest reading lists.

These are the individuals who make up the library community. While many may still prefer the physical branch, the community that is created online "in the stacks" will consist of contributors who share their opinions through reading lists, tags, and reviews as well as the silent type who experience the sense of community through the information shared and created by others. It is not about how many people contribute; rather, it is about how the catalogue can provide an experience that results in fulfilling users' needs. Rather than relying on websites as our main portal, which rarely allows a user to search its pages and content, new library catalogues have the ability to search and organize metadata from the website as well as electronic databases and bibliographic records. The library catalogue can provide a single point of entry to the entire library, with a level of discoverability that library websites alone cannot provide.

What does this mean? Take, for example, the typical library website. There are tabs or linkable buttons that direct the user to the readers' page, the library catalogue, the kids' page, the teens' page, and so on. There are also multiple links providing information on library hours, contact information, and programming. In all, the library website holds a significant amount of information, but it is not organized information. And, it is rarely searchable. However, the library catalogues that are emerging can bring all of the information together—in one single, seamless search. For example, a key word search on the term "cancer" can recall all of the items in the collection on cancer, an upcoming library program on cancer awareness, and all of the community organizations in a specific area. Like other metadata crawlers, library catalogues have the ability to search the library website for information, extract it, and display it in the catalogue. If the possibility to do this is available, why do we ask users to perform numerous searches, first in the website and then in the library catalogue?

The library catalogue as a social space, or online community, draws together elements of trust, interaction and contribution, discoverability, personalization and customization, intuitiveness, belonging, and immediate access to information. In all, they create a level of experience that has been, up until now, found only in the physical library.

As will be discussed throughout the book, social catalogues aren't just about asking users to generate information but also about providing them with a personalized, local experience by taking advantage of the innovative technologies available to us. Using the library catalogue as a social space requires us to rethink our traditional definition of what they library catalogue is or isn't.

FROM INVENTORY TO SOCIAL SPACE; OR, WHAT IS IT, REALLY, THAT USERS WANT?

In an age where everything is immediate and digital, we are seeking to compete in an online world where our communities are accustomed to an environment of immediacy, brevity, and short attention spans. What is it, then, that our users want from us in an online environment?

As librarians, we have often been accused that we use our expertise to decide what is best for our users rather than enhancing our services by soliciting user feedback. The traditional catalogue is a good example of this. According to Gretchen Hoffman, "Although cataloging claims to focus on users, the cataloging field has generally not taken a user-centered approach in research and cataloging standards have not been developed based on an understanding of users' needs" (Hoffman 2009, 632). Many of our cataloguing shortcomings are the result of limited ability to customize bibliographic records, shortcomings with cataloguing software, and an emphasis on productivity and efficiency over customization of records (Hoffman 2009, 632). They have also resulted because of a limited understanding of who our users are and what expectations they have (Hoffman 2009, 633). Accordingly, although we believe that cataloguing standards are based on users' needs, cataloguing policies are determined by the professional expertise of cataloguers who are left to interpret cataloguing rules and guidelines as well as user expectations without the benefit of direct user feedback (Hoffman 2009, 635). All of our library services are based on the same type of practices. Traditionally, when we've seen a need within the library, we've used our professional judgment to create a solution to fill that need. Historically, our collections as well as our reading recommendations were based on the professionals' judgment of quality and users' needs. As well-meaning as that is, our fiction collections as well as graphic novel collections are only starting to lose the stereotypes that were associated with those collections because of our efforts at assuming what is best for our users. As a result, our profession is rather well known for not seeking our users' feedback at the beginning of the process but only after we've implemented changes, started a new service, or completed a project.

Social catalogues are different. These library catalogues have been born out of the expectations of our users. In fact, while library literature has been talking about the need for change in catalogues for over 20 years, it was the emergence of Web 2.0 and users' shift away from library catalogues to more desirable technology that has forced us to listen to our users. We are now trying to use our expertise to answer a new question. How can we get our library to our users rather than attract our users into the library?

In March 2009, OCLC issued a report called *Online Catalogs: What Users and Librarians Want*. While the entire report is based largely on the quality of data within our catalogues, there are key finding in the report that offer a look at why we should redefine library catalogues as social spaces rather than just a tool to access the holdings within the library. The report found the following:

- Users focus on immediacy and attainability of information, which is as important as the experience of finding the information. This includes easier access to all of the information and collections, including online and downloadable content as well as program information, reading recommendations, and availability.
- Users want enriched content, which includes much more than just author, title, and subject but additional information that relates the relevancy of an item to meet his or her needs.
- The relevance of this information must be obvious (OCLC 2009, 11–21).

The expectations of social features are also of key interest. Our users expect to find an interactive aspect to every online destination. This includes the library catalogue. Today's technology invites users to share information in a variety of ways that includes not only generating their own information but also searching information generated by other community members. We see the popularity of these features in Amazon, Flickr, and YouTube.

Despite the fact that OCLC is one of the most recent reports available at the time of this writing, it is already relatively dated because of the release of smartphones, such as Apple's iPhone. Mobile technologies now provide users with yet another way to enter the catalogue and retrieve information. Smartphones are another element in the technology and social software mix. In fact, it emphasizes the idea and need for the library to go to the user rather than have the user come to us. A library's online presence isn't the "destination spot" it was once; rather, it is found through a gateway, pointed out to an individual by a friend, colleague, application, or some type of outside source. The way it is found is through the sharing of reading lists, linkable into the catalogue as well as through link sharing through social networking sites such as Facebook. Other way users are finding and interacting with our libraries is through RSS feeds as well as other users.

With the many gateways through which users are entering our resources, it's important to reconsider how we are organizing those resources. If they are scattered throughout the website and catalogue, users will miss related programs, blog posts, and items in a variety of formats because they are not housed in one centralized and organized location. When users link in to our online presence, we want them to see all of our information, not just portions of it that are stand-alone entities.

Social catalogues are a viable solution for meeting our users' needs and expectations. They are an interactive destination spot that invites users to contribute and that allows them to share their experience through other social technologies. For example, some users of social catalogues use Google books to search inside items as well as share their favourite items by using a wide variety of additional social media formats that include Amazon's wishlist, Del.icio.us, Facebook, Blogger, and Google bookmarks.

IMPACT OF SOCIAL CATALOGUES ON FRONTLINE STAFF: WHY SHOULD I CARE?

If you are reading this book and you are not a cataloguer, it is likely because you understand that the changes occurring in cataloguing, specifically the functions of the library catalogue, will impact frontline staff work flows and professionals throughout the library can take advantage of these catalogues to enhance existing services.

While this topic will be examined more fully later in the book, it is important to understand that changes in one area of our profession are not autonomous. Where at one time advancements in reference, programming, or cataloguing did not greatly impact other areas of the profession, social technologies and their integration into library catalogues will have a deep and profound effect on all areas of library service, from collection development to readers' advisory work and children's programming.

Of course, one can argue that the implementation of the first online catalogue affected the entire profession, so this is not the first time a major advancement in one area of librarianship had a profound impact on work flows and skills throughout the profession. While the implementation of OPACs did impact how frontline staff accessed our collection, the role of the catalogue never changed—it went from a paper-based inventory to an online inventory. The only impact it had on frontline staff was the need to learn how the tool worked. However, next generation library catalogues are taking on new roles, turning cataloguers into readers' advisors, exposing collection development strengths and weaknesses, and adding a level of intuitiveness of use in the library catalogue that will, eventually, remove the need for frontline staff to instruct end users on using the catalogue. Recognizing the amount of remote users in the public library and the need to reach those users, the Kansas City Public Library now offers YouTube videos that instruct patrons on the use of the catalogue based on the types of information they are seeking. This goes beyond a simple instruction on layout and focuses on how to use specific functions for those patrons who still want assistance but don't want to attend training at a library.

Unfortunately, the divide between frontline and backroom staff has resulted in a virtual lack of awareness among many librarians that these social catalogues exist. Or, if they do, they view it as a more attractive version of the existing legacy catalogue, offering some Amazon- and Google-like features. Because of the lack of dialogue and collaboration that often is found in public libraries between the two areas of the profession, it bears repeating that few frontline professionals are aware of the profound impact that social catalogues will have on their area of the profession. In fact, few want to accept that there will be any impact as they continue to create yet another blog for their services, to sit beside the four other blogs created in the library representing other services. Interestingly, it is far easier for many professionals to accept the website as the primary social space, using that as a gateway to the information of the library, than to accept that the library catalogue should play the leading role, with it acting as a gateway to all of our information and enhancing every level of the services we offer.

Social catalogues have the ability to create a community space many frontline staff can take advantage of. One of the themes throughout this book centres on the breaking down of our individual service silos. It is my hope that by the time you have finished reading this book, the need for true collaboration between frontline and backroom staff has become obvious. When asked to comment on the impact social catalogues have on readers' advisors, RAs should be able to make an informed statement regarding its impact on readers' services and the advantages and enhancements that social catalogues offer. This should be the same with every core service area within the library.

CONCLUSION

While core library services, from children's services to reference services and the reintroduction of user services, have grown and changed, the library catalogue has not. While frontline staff have added new content to the library's collective set of information resources, they have done so not through the catalogue but through a variety of stand-alone mediums. This has been accepted not because cataloguers are not capable of organizing the various information being generated and collected by each department but rather because of the limitations of legacy catalogues and a lack of collaboration among frontline and backroom staff. Websites that include programming information, library events, and branch hours also include links to various blogs and wikis that store relevant and valuable information to users. Unfortunately, this information is not as well organized or accessible as it could be. Social catalogues take the library branch to the user and provide a front door as well as multiple entry points to give the user immediate access to all the information and expertise a library has to offer.

If we continue to implement self-contained social software into our library practices, there will be an abundance of opportunities to be where the users are but no way to navigate from one service to another. We already see this with the use of a different blog for each library service, linking back to the main library website but not the catalogue and not the electronic collections or even to each other. A social catalogue brings all of this information into one searchable and well-organized space. It is a space that provides gateways that lead from books and downloadable materials to local newspaper article, blog posts, or library programs. The only limitation is the traditional definition of the library catalogue: our own creativity based on what the library catalogue is versus what it is becoming.

REFERENCES

Hoffman, Gretchen L. "Meeting Users' Needs in Cataloging: What Is the Right Thing to Do?" *Cataloging & Classification Quarterly* (2009): 631–41. Accessed August 20, 2009, doi: 10.1080/01639370903111999.
OCLC. "Online Catalogs: What Users and Librarians Want." *OCLC Report*. 2009.

CHAPTER 2

Exploring Next Generation Catalogues

Without an understanding of the concepts and structure behind next generation catalogues and their features, it might be difficult imagining any library catalogue becoming a collaborative, interactive tool extending beyond our physical branch into users homes or wherever they are. Up until now, this type of interaction with our patrons has been possible only through integrating stand-alone Web 2.0 tools into our websites or using outside social networking tools as a way to reach our users. This is exhibited through our use of reference chat, Facebook pages, blogs, and Twitter accounts. However, multiple Twitter accounts, toggling from one Facebook page to another, or following a variety of blogs generated from one library but each representing a difference service has been a clumsy way of trying to reach our users and provide them with the interactive services they are looking for. While not a criticism of our current practice, we have been limited in our ability to streamline our interactive and collaborative tools because of the traditional limitations placed on us by limited resources and vendor products.

While next generation catalogues can improve on many of our existing social networking efforts, it has to be stressed that many of the thoughts and ideas in this book are also looking toward the future and not just what they can do today. As a result, while social catalogues will enhance existing practices, they are not yet able to assist in answering every need in the remote, social environment in which we are currently working.

Throughout this chapter, the terms "social catalogues" and "next generation catalogues" will be used interchangeably. Another term, "discovery tool," will also be introduced. Discovery tools are social catalogues, but rather than replacing a library catalogue with a product that includes social and intuitive features, they are interfaces that overlay our legacy catalogues. As a result, discovery tools allow a library to keep their existing catalogue. For many public libraries, this is the only way they are able to acquire a social catalogue because of the time, expertise, cost, and additional resources required to implement or transition into a completely new catalogue. While resources and expertise are still required to implement a discovery tool, in most cases it is not a complete migration of an entire catalogue and its data to another system. As a result, by acquiring a discovery tool or social interface, libraries are able to provide new, intuitive interfaces that provide a level of customization and enhancement they may not otherwise be able to provide. Throughout this chapter and the remainder of the book, discovery tools as well as stand-alone next generation catalogues will be discussed. As an example, the social catalogue Endeca, which will be discussed early in this chapter, is an example of a social catalogue, or a stand-alone catalogue, which replaces a library's existing catalogue. However, products such as Encore and AquaBrowser, which are also discussed in this chapter, are examples of discovery tools that overlay and provide an intuitive, customizable interface for a library's existing catalogue.

WHAT, EXACTLY, IS A SOCIAL CATALOGUE?

Today, the technology and software we use to implement next generation catalogues are developed specifically for libraries. However, when the University of North Carolina implemented the first version of a "social catalogue" in libraries shortly after Endeca was made available to libraries in 2004, a significant amount of customization was necessary for use in our environment. A popular choice for commercial websites such as Barnes & Noble, Home Depot, and Wal-Mart, Endeca was founded in 1999 and in 2006 was awarded a patent that covered its "hierarchical data driven navigation system and method for information retrieval" (Breeding 2007, 19). Or it can be more easily described as "guided navigation," a phrase coined by Marshall Breeding in the *Library Technology Report* issue titled "Next Generation Library Catalogs" (Breeding 2007, 19). Endeca provided libraries with an alternative to heavily restrictive library software. Its strengths include a highly customizable interface, relevancy-ranked search results, and in-house control over options for search configurations. When launched, the University of North Carolina's library catalogue became the premier example of the future of the library catalogue because it provided many of the popular features that our users had become accustomed to in commercial sites. However, with the significant amount of resources required to customize and afford such a catalogue, it remained out of reach for many public and academic libraries.

The library catalogue at the University of North Carolina exhibited many of the features that are now the foundation for next generation catalogues. However, at the time of Endeca's implementation at the University of North Carolina, the Web 2.0 movement had barely begun, and online social networking was only in its infancy. Today, social catalogues have built on and improved the intuitive catalogue model that first appeared in libraries less than a decade ago. In addition to intuitive interfaces, control over search configurations and relevancy-ranked results, interactive features have been added that allow user-generated information within our catalogues and a level of sharing with external user tools that did not exist in the past.

Today, next generation catalogues are interactive, collaborative library catalogues that are defined by their intuitive interfaces that often allow users to search the library's holdings, additional data sources, and user-generated information in a single search. They are recognizable by their transparent ranking of results, invitation to allow users to generate and interact with information, and the ability to share information from the catalogue through external social media. However, these catalogues are not simply defined by the software that a library obtains from a vendor or through open source. While this chapter focuses on vendor-created social catalogues that provide an "out-of-the-box" social catalogue (discovery tool) for libraries to use, a social catalogue is more than just another piece of software. Next generation catalogues are a vision for the future of public libraries that extends beyond that of our physical branches. They promote patron interaction with staff and each other while allowing users to find the answers to their information needs, to manipulate the data to fit their needs, and to do this through whatever electronic device they wish to use. As a result, the development and future of social catalogues focus on the experience of users' information and social needs outside of the library, providing them with the same if not better experience than they would have in the physical library.

When reading professional literature, talking with colleagues, or attending conferences, we hear many names of next generation catalogues mentioned. They include Endeca, Primo, Encore, Polaris, AquaBrowser, and BiblioCommons. In fact, they tend to be grouped together in a generic social catalogue category. Like our integrated library systems, next generation catalogues are not all the same. While they share core characteristics and features that include elements such as a single search box, relevancy ranking, and the ability to customize search configurations, the software varies from one vendor to another or one open-source platform to another. As a result, there is no single discovery tool or social catalogue that will offer all of the features we'd like. However, each catalogue continues to evolve and change as the software is enhanced, and it's important to know what the common features are in these catalogues. They include the following:

- Intuitive interfaces
- Enhanced searching capability
- Relevancy-ranked results

- Faceted navigation, including decisions on the content of the facets
- Fuzzy logic or "did you mean ... ?" search assistance
- User-generated content, such as tagging, rating, and reviewing items as well as creating personalized reading lists
- Searchable user-generated tags, reviews, and comments
- Searchable book summaries
- RSS feeds for following user- and staff-created reading lists
- Customizable interfaces, including in-house customization of format icons, choice of instructive text language, layout, and content creation for help instructions
- Ability to offer interface in a variety of languages
- Tag clouds/word clouds that provide a discovery path based a variety of data elements that include translations, proximity terms, synonyms, and popularity

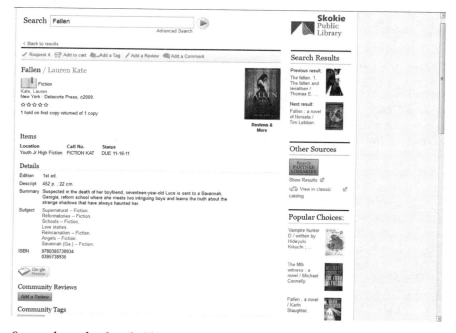

Screenshot of a detailed bibliographic record in AquaBrowser, as seen at Skokie Public Library (http://encore.skokielibrary.info/iii/encore/record/ C__Rb1609566__SFallen__Ff%3Afacetmediatype%3Af%3Af%3AFiction%3A%3A__P0%2C3__Orightresult__X5?lang=eng&suite=cobalt).

Some of these features may be familiar to many professionals. However, in an effort to understand the extent to which social cataloguing features surpass our legacy catalogues, several of the terms need to be examined. In particular, the concepts behind faceted navigation, single search and sign-in, and user-generated information will be explored.

FACETED NAVIGATION

Faceted navigation is a way of refining search results by pulling out key concepts from the items that were retrieved in the search and presenting them in a tool bar as options for narrowing down results. This assists users in understanding and refining search results to fit their needs or interests rather than forcing them to create a complicated search string to draw out relevant information. In other words, it is a way of filtering results, based on an original search term or terms. For example, if you're interested in exercising, you may enter the term "exercise" in your search box. From exercise, additional options would be provided. They could include different types of exercises, the many formats you can choose from (DVDs, books, and community program), specific authors/instructors, date ranges, and so on. Each time an additional option is chosen, further options are provided, allowing you to "drill down" to a specific item or items.

However, it must be understood that the facets, or filtering options, are only as good as the content in the bibliographic records or additional data sources from which information is being mined. The reason is that the information presented in the facets is derived from data sources such as a library's bibliographic and authority records and even the library website. As a result, faceted navigation allows us to pull out and sort the rich data that, up until the development of these catalogues, have been undiscoverable or unsearchable. Faceted navigation cannot draw comparisons or conclusions about data, but it can group like concepts and information together.

Options for facets in catalogues include formats, publication dates, performers/authors, targeted audiences, topics, subjects, genres, languages, subtitles, and so on. If the information is available in the bibliographic or authority databases in your integrated library system (ILS), they can be made available in facets. However, the degree to which the facets are useful relies heavily on the quality of MARC records, or cataloguing expertise, in your library. If the data contained within bibliographic records are not uniform or consistent, the facets provided to users for refining their search will also be inconsistent. Facets are not restricted to information found only in the library catalogue. They can also include outside sources, such as external databases (e.g., a newspaper index), or websites that might include blogs, the library website, or local institutions' websites.

Many libraries find that the implementation of features such as this exposes many of their catalogue's shortcomings. This is not the fault of the library or cataloguing department but rather the result of years of emphasis on cataloguing with an eye to quantity over quality that many cataloguing departments have been pressured into. If libraries do not have in-house cataloguers, it is often the result of receiving records from various vendors or

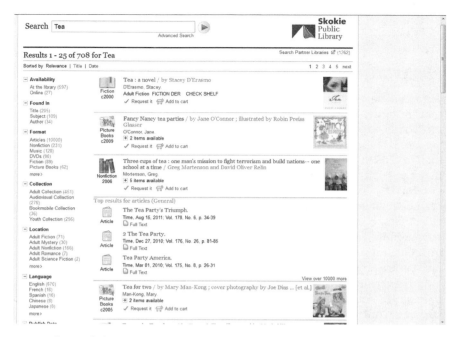

Screenshot of the popular public library discovery tool Encore, implemented at Skokie Public Library. Customization is a strong characteristic of these catalogues (http://encore.skokielibrary.info/iii/encore/search/C__STea__Orightresult__U1?lang=eng&suite=cobalt).

from copy cataloguing, with no standard or uniform cataloguing practices providing content contained within the records.

While the quality of a library's bibliographic data plays an essential role in the success of faceted navigation, libraries do not have to give up this powerful searching tool if their data are less than perfect. There are a number of ways to "clean up" machine-readable cataloging (MARC) records so that faceted navigation can work successfully within a catalogue. MarcEdit is an example of a type of software that can be used to make mass editing changes to MARC records. MarcEdit was developed by Terry Reese, a fellow librarian, and is available as a free download. This software allows for changes to MARC records, including altering, adding, or deleting content. If your records are not created in-house or not controlled in-house, making mass editing impossible, there are other options. If your library receives records supplied by vendors, most vendors are receptive to enhancing the bibliographic data provided within the MARC records of the items purchased. It's important to work with these vendors so that if you are receiving data from various sources they are standardized as much as possible. And, of course, in-house cataloguers can assist in cleaning up authority records or bibliographic records.

No matter the quality of data within a library's bibliographic and authority records, faceted navigation will find its shortcomings. All libraries should expect that a level of data enhancement and cleanup is necessary to successfully provide faceted navigation. However, the benefits of having this type of navigation are worth the effort. Imagine having a patron ask for feature DVDs from 2009 that are in English but have Chinese subtitles. How will staff go about finding this information? While a handful of key words may assist in finding some of the items within the library that match the collection, more often than not, films in Chinese with English subtitles will be retrieved with the same frequency as items in English with Chinese subtitles. However, faceted navigation will allow a staff member or patron to find results that meet this query without typing in a single word. First, the format DVD will be chosen, followed by the year and the language. Drilling down with facets, a user can then choose "Chinese" under the refine option for subtitles and be given a list of films to choose from that indicate whether it is a feature or nonfeature film.

SINGLE SEARCH BOX

Like the single search box in Google, many social catalogues use a single search box that can search any data source, website, or harvested data set that the library chooses to incorporate into its sources of data retrieval. In other words, when performing a search query, a next generation catalogue can retrieve results not only from the library catalogue but also from data sources such as the library website or other identified websites chosen by the library. As a result, library hours, programs, pages from the library website, or local events in the area geared toward particular users, as well as holdings on a particular search query, will be retrieved, all in one search. This greatly reduces the need for toggling from one page to another on the library website or local organizations' websites and catalogues, instead retrieving all of the relevant information in one place for staff and patrons.

USER ACCOUNTS AND USER-GENERATED INFORMATION

Perhaps the most coveted yet problematic feature (or desired feature) for social catalogues is single sign-in. As users explore and discover in these new catalogues, searches can be interrupted if they are forced to reauthenticate every time users wish to place holds or take advantage of features that require a patron log-in. Rather, users want searches to be remembered (as well as their account information) so that they can place holds on items, navigate through new searches, and place holds again in a single, authenticated session. While creators of next generation catalogues recognize this as a desirable feature, there are several issues that arise from attempting to implement it successfully.

While commercial sites have been more successful at remembering log-in information during multiple transactions in a single session, library catalogues have not. Many of the issues surrounding this deal with privacy and limitations placed upon libraries by their ILSs and vendors. For example, within branches, most computers clear the user information after a hold is placed, or they "time-out" after a set period of time. This is to prevent new users of that computer from accessing or being signed on as a previous user. However, in many cases, next generation catalogues are overlays that sit on top of the public catalogue component of our ILSs. This means that whatever authentication the originating ILS uses, now it has to go through the discovery layer to the underlying ILS. In most cases, this can be done by integrating a tool such as EZproxy into the discovery layer. However, if there are firewall issues for accessing the library's server or integration issues, this can create further problems, the most prominent being untimely log-outs, difficulties setting log-in parameters, or restricted remote access of the library catalogue.

Libraries that integrate next generation catalogues supplied by the same vendor as that of their current ILS or that implement new ILSs that provide social catalogues within their product tend not to face this issue or at least do so less frequently. As with any product, if you use the same vendor for all of your services, compatibility is easier to achieve because the products have been made to complement each other and integrate together.

With concerns over privacy, user accounts are another issue that professionals need to address when faced with choosing a social catalogue. While some catalogues integrate the library patron's account with user-generated activity, many other social catalogues do not.

User accounts are a concern to professionals because of the very public side of social catalogues. For users to freely and openly add content in the catalogue with or without absolute anonymity is debatable. When a user's library account is linked to their user-generated information, library staff are allowed to see and attribute the content being generated to an individual user. For purposes of ferreting out users who abuse the freedom of content creation by adding inappropriate words or inflammatory content, this is viewed as an acceptable and professional practice. Other professionals rather ask users to create a separate, freestanding account to contribute information, thereby creating total anonymity. To control any abuses, stop words created in a type of "black list" monitor information being generated, blocking inappropriate terms or reviews from being published within the catalogue. This second system is based on the current social media model, where users are responsible for their behaviour and monitoring others as well, with the expectation that most users are good intentioned and that abuse will be minimal.

There is no right or wrong answer to how user accounts are accessed or integrated into next generation catalogues, but the choice of how this is done is decided on by the catalogue that is chosen. Next generation catalogues do not provide an either/or option. However, given the different nuances of each catalogue or discovery layer, it is likely that the catalogue that most attracts you also provides the type of user account setup you prefer. Like any product, next generation catalogues are developed with specific beliefs or intentions. As such, each catalogue bears its own mark, and while certain commonalities are shared, they are different. What is interesting is that despite the many well-developed and excellent social catalogues available that are all equal but different, each library professional will have a preference.

ADDITIONAL FEATURES

There are also additional features found in next generation catalogues that are less standard and most often unique to only one or two of these catalogues. They include the following:

- Customizable user accounts
- Ability to share catalogue data, such as specific bibliographic records of favourite items, with other social networking sites
- Compatibility with mobile devices, including a specialized mobile platform
- Ability to search additional data sources, included the library website, locally created databases, and websites

Overall, there is a wealth of information and features available in next generation catalogues that are not possible to provide in our legacy catalogues. In addition to these features, there are backend statistics that provide staff with unique, user-focused and community-focused information that reflects community needs, interests, and trends. The uses for this information and the impact that statistics and social catalogues have on our core library services are discussed in the coming chapters. It is also important to note that, similar to our legacy or classic catalogues, these new social catalogues allow for additional social media add-ons or vendor products that also enrich a user's experience in the catalogue. Chat widgets for reference and readers' advisory within the catalogue as well as vendor products that supply search inside features, cover art, and book summaries and reviews from journals can seamlessly be integrated into these social catalogues. Two additional and noteworthy features that are gaining popularity in integrating with next generation catalogues are federated searching and readers' advisory–generated content.

With a single search box, federated searching allows a user to explore all of the library's physical and virtual holdings in one search. Specifically, it allows a user to search a library's subscription databases from within the library catalogue. Often hard to locate on a library website or neglected because of its lack of visibility, federated searching can be integrated into next generation catalogues in a variety of ways. Because of the customizable capabilities of this software, you can decide where and, to some extent, how the results should appear on the catalogue interface. However, this technology is still in its infancy. As a result, there are limitations that do prohibit the federated search results from displaying within the bibliographic records results lists. But even with these limitations, patrons and staff are no longer forced to toggle between a variety of windows, performing the same search multiple times to retrieve all of the relevant results. With the integration of federated searching into next generation catalogues, all of the library's information is found in one, single search.

WHO OWNS YOUR DATA?

In a world where information flows freely and we're slowly shedding the limitations of our existing ILSs, it's easy to take for granted that the statistics and data on which many of our services rely on is ours. We can run reports on it, use it to justify new programs and services, observe trends, and justify (or don't) the existence of extra staff, resources, or departments. Being able to observe dead-end searches, where our users are coming from, and the amount of interaction (in a variety of ways) that patrons are interacting with the catalogue is exciting and informative.

With new discovery tools and social catalogues, library management and cataloguers are taking it for granted that the same freedom we've had with our ILS data carries over to these new tools. However, that isn't always the case. And, just like the many complaints about limitations we've had with our ILSs, there are limitations on the accessibility of data and types of statistics kept by discovery tools.

While many professionals are already pushing for a next generation catalogue—and maybe even a next next generation catalogue (perhaps we can think of something easier?)—many of us are still navigating through the intricacies of implementing our first "next" generation catalogue. In all of the excitement of what is *now* and what is coming with catalogues, especially the features (potential and "shiny new" characteristics), it's easy to overlook why we're implementing them.

And, while it has been a habit in many public libraries simply to say "we're implementing it because people want it," there are problems with this method. To get to the point where we know that "people want it," we need to look at data—surveys, user groups, usage patterns, and a variety of other data sources. To prove that the new catalogue is successful, we need more data—surveys, user groups, usage patterns, and so on.

But what happens when you don't have access to your data? What if the data provided to you are limited or restricted? What if their usage and access are restricted by your vendor? What if the data that concern you most, such as statistics on social features in catalogues, are missing?

Data are powerful. How data are manipulated (and I'm using this word on purpose) for reports, how they are presented, and what they can show you is vital to properly evaluating a discovery tool and its success/failure at your library.

You may want to look at your statistics throughout the month rather than your vendor providing you with a single report at the end of the month. If we rely on our vendors for data on the usage of their product, we cannot guarantee that we are receiving the "whole picture" or just the statistics that positively reflect the product. Overall, it's comforting to know that the data belong to your library and that you can share it with whomever you choose and pull out a variety of details that may appear useless to someone else.

Because many discovery tools sit on top of your ILS, you can't rely on the data from your ILS to provide you with statistics on usage of the features in your social catalogue. And these are the key features behind why a discovery tool/social catalogue was implemented. If we can't see if these features are being used or if the usage changes over time, we can't justify their existence. And we certainly can't provide supporting statistical evidence to vendors when we ask them to change, alter, or create additional features for our catalogues.

When choosing a discovery tool, social catalogue, or whatever you call it at your library, ask questions and read the fine print. Who owns your data? How much access will you have to it? Can you share it? While it's easy to get caught up in the wealth of opportunities and potential benefits that next generation catalogues offer, don't forget to ask vital questions that will assist you in examining the justification of their existence.

DISCOVERY TOOLS IN PUBLIC LIBRARIES

The number of open-source and vendor-supplied next generation catalogues continues to increase. Because of the variety of discovery tools available to libraries, it is important to take the time to examine which catalogue is best for your library and your community's needs. As with the development of many technologies within the library environment, the development of social catalogues has experienced an interesting evolution. As the software grew, so did certain specialties among the technologies to fit the needs of the users. While the University of North Carolina introduced the Endeca product into their catalogue and many other academic libraries have adopted WorldCat, most public libraries have not followed suit by using the same solutions. Endeca, WorldCat, and Primo are three next generation catalogue platforms that are not known to be popular among public libraries. In fact, while all three can be implemented in a public library setting, their features are designed to accommodate an academic library environment and the needs of those users.

For many, the cost of these catalogues and demand on public library resources are prohibitive to public libraries, whereas the funds and technological support and expertise may be found in an academic setting. For others, it is the features they offer, such as additional citation features or even assistance for generating bibliographic citations, while falling short of public library users' needs, such as simple customization or implementation of readers' services features. Why have some next generation catalogues become popular in academic libraries but not in public libraries? Likely, the most simple response is to say cost, demands on in-house resources, and perception. Products are born in many cases out of a need. While some vendors targeted the academic audience for their product, other vendors saw a unique and different need in the public library environment and decided to market to us. Knowing which discovery tools have been created with public library needs in mind assists in understanding why certain features were developed and whether the software will continue to develop in ways that will suit our unique community's needs. At this time, some of the most popular next generation catalogues in public libraries include Polaris, AquaBrowser, and Encore. In Canada, one of the most popular products is BiblioCommons, which is steadily gaining popularity in public libraries in the United States as well. These next generation catalogues have targeted the public library market, demonstrating the ease with which the interface can be implemented and customized to suit a particular library's needs.

As with any technology, it is important to understand the foundation behind its development. Some next generation catalogues have been created with academic users in mind, including the resources that are required for implementation, while others have been specifically created to serve the needs of public library communities. Exploring all of the social catalogues available for implementation is beyond the scope of this publication. However, with an examination of the common features that social catalogues offer, it is possible to discern the many options and enhancements not offered by traditional legacy catalogues. While each next generation catalogue varies in its features, strengths, and deficits, the constant in all of these catalogues is the idea that library catalogues are more than just inventories; they are social, collaborative spaces that allows users to share, collaborate, and answer their information needs. But more than that, they are intuitive catalogues that provide a sense of ownership to users, allowing all of us to use the catalogue and information therein to match our needs.

WHICH CATALOGUE IS RIGHT FOR YOUR LIBRARY?

Now that your library has decided on a social catalogue, how are you going to decide which one? What if you don't even know about them? While this book should assist in navigating through the intricacies of social catalogues and their future in public libraries, it cannot provide an examination into every feature, benefit, or concern that we have for their acquisition and implementation.

Like any software, next generation catalogues have their problems. You can find a number of articles discussing the technical difficulties or support issues that have been encountered for each solution. However, all social catalogues and, in particular, discovery tools offer a package that many libraries can no longer afford to ignore, especially if we want to compete with information giants such as Google, Amazon, and LibraryThing. Without switching to a new ILS, discovery tools allow us to implement key features within the catalogue that include a "did you mean?" function, spelling recommendations, search results with no dead ends, social tagging, list making, review writing, and user ratings. We can finally include tag clouds and federated searching in a single search box. Given the relative newness of this software, their features are continually being enhanced and expanded. And, unlike an ILS, you are not "stuck" with a solution if you want to change it.

If you've been contemplating the idea of implementing a discovery tool in your library, here are some steps that will help with the process:

1. Look at what our competitors are doing. Check out other libraries and play with Amazon, LibraryThing, Facebook, and other social catalogues, networks, and software. What are they doing? Has it been successful and why?

2. Research. At this time, don't pigeonhole yourself into looking at your options. This research should be a bit broader. What are people saying about social catalogues? Are their surveys available regarding the use of social catalogues and their features? Stories of successes and failures? What about lessons learned or blog posts of firsthand experiences? Even if you start researching with only a basic understanding of discovery tools, this process will introduce you to the software available as well as studies, research, opinions, and surveys available for review. Why reinvent the wheel?

3. Now that you've got a good foundation of knowledge on social catalogues, it's time to consider the following:
   - Proprietary versus open-source software
   - Solution requirements (What would you like the software to do? What does it have to do?)
   - Who are your users and what are their needs?
   - Budget, staff resources, and time line

By this point, you've probably narrowed down your choices to a handful of options. Call those vendors or software developers to ask them about their product. Many times, they'll even send you sample requests for proposals to assist you if you're required to draft one. If they do, this will give you a good idea of what other libraries require of their software. This is a great time to ask about special customized features or to address concerns you have about something you've read. And, of course, contact other libraries. Don't be afraid to speak with colleagues at other libraries about their experiences or opinions.

CONCLUSION

While this chapter provides insight into social catalogues, what they are, and their features, it is by no means an exhaustive study of what is available. If we take a look at the library literature over the past 20 or even 30 years, there are many articles talking about what a library catalogue could and should be. It should be an instrument used to find all of the library's resources. It should be a catalogue that invites user input and suggestions. It should be a place to recommend books to other readers. The "It" is now the social catalogue. "It" is a group of next generation catalogues that has realized a dream and a vision among the library profession for over a quarter of a century. When we think about the old card catalogues, we can remember the pencil markings made by patrons, indicating likes, dislikes, or recommendations. This is something that patrons have wanted as well—and were doing without our support when we used card catalogues. However, technology is now allowing us to give users, including staff, the library catalogue that many professionals have been hoping to see throughout their careers: a physical extension of the library branch in an online environment.

Throughout this book, ideas about why next generation catalogues are important are explored. Examining the concept that library catalogues can become a community space and why they need to be explored as such a space can be accomplished only by seeing what the current group of next generation catalogues offer. It is quite promising to see that despite have only found its first implementation in 2006, next generation catalogues have progressed and developed rapidly. This provides a good indication that there is recognition of the value these catalogues serve and the important roles they will play in the future of our ever-changing library environment.

REFERENCE

Breeding, Marshall. "Next Generation Library Catalogs." *Library Technology Reports: Expert Guides to Systems and Services.* ALA Techsource. 2007.

CHAPTER 3

Controversies and Concerns Surrounding Next Generation Catalogues

When my thoughts and ideas were first introduced to the larger cataloguing community, thoughtful, heated, and very interesting conversations arose. I was scared and thrilled at the same time to see that while many cataloguers were open to the idea of a library catalogue becoming a community space, others had serious misgivings. However, several themes and patterns emerged in these conversations. Public librarians and public library management teams appear to be more willing to explore the possibilities of a library catalogue stepping outside of its traditional role than academic professionals (both those who teach at library schools and those who work in academic libraries). While this isn't meant to be a sweeping generalization, it is true that in a public setting we appear to be more willing to adopt or experiment with new trends and to jump in with both feet. This may be due to the fact that public libraries allow for more freedom in content, while an academic environment is just that: academic. It might also be due to the directions or mandates we have to fulfill, support from our management and staff, or vision for what we believe our users want or need from our catalogues.

Following the professional discussion lists, it's apparent that many of the changes and enhancements that next generation catalogues provide are often mutated into another conversation that involves how our metadata should and can be doing the things that next generation catalogues have already achieved. Rather than understanding that these catalogues can complement our cataloguing practices, academics are often challenging our own cataloguing practices and how they can accomplish these same principles without taking advantage of technology. At other times, whether it's through lack of understanding, background knowledge, or resistance, discussions examining the library catalogue turning into a social and community space are mutated into statements such as "The library has always been a social space" and, basically, "How is this idea a new one?"

A colleague and friend following one of these conversations over a discussion list offered some words of wisdom that capture a large part of the controversies surrounding next generation catalogues: "I seem to detect in this conversation a divide between those who live on the Net and can see its possibilities and those who may read extensively about and even dabbled in the Net but don't live there."

Often in my conversations with colleagues and professionals, I am brought back to my friend's words, as they tend to hold true. That isn't to say that all professionals who question the functions and use of next generation catalogues fall into one of these two groups. But, as you read this book, ask yourself if you fall into one of these categories or if your managers or colleagues do. Understanding the depth of knowledge or experience your colleagues have on the Internet and in the social environment will help you in determining how to address concerns and barriers as well as understanding their positions on the value and use of next generation catalogues.

During the writing of this book, there was a conversation taking place on the *AUTOCAT* discussion list called "nice step toward what a catalog can become" ("Nice Step toward What a Catalog Can Become," 2011). It reinforces the fact that there are well-educated, informed professionals on both sides of the discussion regarding what a next generation catalogue can and should do. In particular, it appears that while some practicing professionals can see only the shortcomings of these catalogues, focusing primarily on a compromise of certain functions, others see the current and future potential that these catalogues offer. There also seems to be a mistaken impression by many of our colleagues that the iteration we see at one library is the only option available to us. This is a mistake many of us make, not understanding that these catalogues are highly customizable and that much of the interface and display features are the result of choices made by the library. This discussion is important, however, in providing a distinct example of how professionals—and specifically cataloguers—have differing opinions on what the future of the library catalogue looks like and that there are as many professionals who hesitate at the thought of these catalogues as those who support them. However, when reading the discussion, it soon becomes apparent that many of the hesitators do so because they do not have a full understanding of how next generation catalogues work (e.g., options for customization), or many are trenched in cataloguing tradition and as a result appear to find only the "shortcomings" of function. Many point out that it appears that existing functions, such as the browsing function in catalogues, have been compromised in an effort to provide flashy, social features. Unfortunately, the features that cataloguers adamantly point to as necessary haven't been proven to be essential to users. We are all aware that our current catalogues aren't that successful among today's users and that the rate of dead-end searching or unsuccessful searches among our users is high, especially in public libraries. We are faced with this truth in our libraries on a day-to-day basis.

Understanding that even the trendsetters in the cataloguing world are not in agreement over the future of the library catalogue and what it looks like is important to understanding why I've written this chapter. If a cataloguer wants to implement a next generation catalogue in his library, it can be frustrating when frontline colleagues can see only the shortcomings and vice versa. Frontline staff who are also frustrated with the library catalogue may want to look for alternate solutions but are faced with naysayers in the cataloguing department.

This chapter will examine the most common reasons that professionals, both frontline staff and backroom staff, question the use of next generation catalogues as a collaborative and social tool. It complements the following chapter, which explores the relationships between frontline and backroom staff and the collaborative relationship that is necessary among all staff within the library to make a social catalogue as well as any future technological trends for offering remote services successful. Broken down into three categories, the first section of this chapter will address concerns and positions expressed by professionals that represent opinions from the entire profession, while the other two sections will address concerns from frontline public service staff and cataloguers, respectively.

THE PLAY SPACES ON OUR LIBRARY WEBSITE DO NOT HAVE TO BE HOUSED WITHIN THE CATALOGUE

Even before we leave library school, we start asking questions about how our profession provides certain services, and we're full of ideas for improving those services. But something happens when we enter the profession and start practicing. A key phrase that newcomers, trendsetters and movers and shakers are often confronted with is "That's the way we've always done it." Those colleagues who express this sentiment shouldn't be frowned on; they are usually professionals who, like you, have great ideas but have learned from past experiences that it is difficult to influence and change longtime practices. As in any profession, it is easier to half implement or halfheartedly change a service than to take a leap of faith and drastically overhaul a practice. How many of you have had ideas that became watered-down versions of their originally forms, only to see later on that a library in another town has adopted your original idea successfully?

The point of this is to understand that, even when faced with criticism or hesitation among your colleagues, it isn't so much that they doubt what you're trying to do but rather that they do know that change demands a lot of resources and an open mind. In libraries, most decisions for changes in a service or practice require numerous steps and involve large teams from a variety of service areas. Because of the time, energy, politics, and compromise often required to implement change, it is natural to come across common excuses, lack of interest, or resistance.

One of the most common arguments against creating a social catalogue involves the popular belief that a catalogue is nothing more than an inventory with no use outside that of its traditional role. Instead, it's the library's website that's the "play" area and discovery resource. There's no denying that in most if not all public libraries, the website has been the main hub of the virtual branch, or "e-library." With the ability to customize websites without the confines and restrictions we face with our integrated library systems (ILSs), it's been a natural play area for our patrons, and it has been, for the most part, an overwhelming success. However, that isn't to say that the catalogue can't become a play area too. In fact, we can reasonably argue that the library catalogue should and will become the primary play area, directory and discovery resource in the future.

When professionals argue that the library catalogue should be left alone to continue on its traditional path, I always ask, "Why?" Just because something hasn't been done before doesn't mean the idea can't be explored. And why can't the catalogue also become a play area? Can there only be one? If users do not make a distinction between the online catalogue and the website, why do we have such strong opinions against the catalogue becoming the primary destination spot? With a seamless integration between the two, we should consider the tool which allows for the most discoverability to be the face of our remote services. Unfortunately, for many professionals, two concerns arise when suggesting that the catalogue can become a play area. The catalogue removes the need for a website or the usefulness of a website, and the catalogue becomes a dumping ground for information outside of our collection.

Both of these reactions often stem from self-preservation. The webmaster to the library website may feel that his position and expertise is on the line. Other professionals simply misunderstand or choose to misunderstand how additional data can be implemented and retrieved within the catalogue. As a result, they feel a need to "shut down" the conversation by making extreme comments to scare away colleagues who are interested or to put you, an advocate of this idea, on the defense. However, before we bite back, it is important to take a step back and examine these statements. After all, they do represent the thoughts of many professionals, and if they do not understand the concepts and structure behind social catalogues, their concerns are legitimate and should be treated as such.

Whenever an idea is presented that suggests "mashing up" one service into another, the professionals on the receiving end of the mash-up get nervous. What this means is that, if you're a readers' advisor and the catalogue manager tells you that the catalogue can assist or even take over providing reading recommendations within the catalogue, readers' advisors get nervous. It's because of the "what happens to me" factor. Rather than looking at an opportunity that allows readers' advisors to collaborate with the catalogue to enhance RA services to patrons, many will see it as a new idea that jeopardizes their position. I once had a well-respected readers' advisory guru tell me that it's so hard to let go of traditional roles. These roles have helped define services and while there are numerous benefits that often result from change, they can't see or imagine those other possibilities. The same is true with the catalogue becoming a play space in addition to or instead of the library website.

To me, it's not a matter of "either/or" but rather "in addition to." The catalogue serves one purpose, the website another. There are many webmasters and technology gurus who indicate that the website will eventually become our library catalogue, but, in truth, each has a role to play, and they complement each other. Up until now, however, it's only been the website that has been the central hub of a library's activities and as a gateway into the catalogue and many services offered. But what if the catalogue became the main Web page for the public library? The catalogue isn't replacing the many Web pages and the website; it is simply becoming the new library doors through which our users enter.

MORE INTUITIVE INTERFACES, WEAKER SEARCH FUNCTIONS

Even in the early 2000s, when vendors began offering the use of enriched content in library catalogues such as cover art and reviews, a cry went up among library professionals that while catalogues were being transformed to reflect our e-commerce competitors, functionality and an enrichment of functions were being ignored. Today, the same argument is used when discussing next generation catalogues—and these arguments have merit. While social catalogues provide markedly enhanced features, are more attractive, and have undergone a significant makeover to provide users with more information more quickly, there is a very basic function in many catalogues that has been ignored with the advent of these catalogues: the search function.

Little can be argued about the enhanced intuitiveness and usability of next generation catalogues. With features such as "did you mean" options when entering misspelled terms, visual indications of format and item availability and the ability to refine searches with entering additional search queries, the "user friendliness" of library catalogues, and the wealth of information now provided to users, these catalogues reflect much of what the entire library profession has been requesting of our online catalogues for some time. However, with the advent and promotion of social interaction, usability, and "Google-like" interfaces, the traditional functions of our catalogue, such as advanced search options, call number sorting, and author and/or subject browse capabilities, have been compromised.

One of the strongest complaints that library staff currently have with next generation catalogues is that most lack the ability to perform author and subject browses. This is definitely a shortcoming that has gained some ire among reference and front desk staff in public libraries. And it is a legitimate concern. So much of our literature focuses on what users want from our library catalogues that we forget that users represent our public users *and* our staff. If new catalogues have been created that are meeting only some of our users' needs but compromising the needs of others, there are design flaws that need to be addressed. But it's not unexpected that they won't be. New technology takes time to develop as benchmarks are set and measured.

Because a large percentage of social catalogues operate as overlays to existing ILSs, we aren't as limited in demands for enhancements and upgrades as when we're faced with a large, multifaceted vendor-based ILS. One of the strengths of using a social catalogue is that the interface is easier to change, and vendors are often eager to do so to enhance their product. This is not only for you but also for future clients where they can then offer increasingly cutting-edge "out-of-the-box" library packages that include the most up-to-date enhancements. Also, with the availability of multiple competitive overlays or "interfaces," it isn't as difficult or as hard on library resources to switch to another platform, unlike integrating to a new ILS. Social catalogue interfaces and their functions reflect the observations, comments, suggestions, and improvements as new technologies are developed and interoperability with our existing ILSs improves. But it takes time. While it's easy to criticize social catalogues and this targeted weakness in design, it is easy to forget all of the enhancements and improvements that have been made to our existing catalogues with these interfaces. And it has to be remembered that if our profession is still asking each other, "What is it that users want in and from the catalogue?" vendors are also struggling with this question. What they've designed, up until now, largely reflects our professional literature, outside commercial-based evidence and our own opinions about what the catalogue should be, taking for granted but never explicitly saying that the existing features of legacy catalogues should also be improved.

Also, it is important to note that while many of these new catalogues do not offer author and/or subject browse options, they all offer a level of discovery and refinement that our legacy catalogues never did.

FRONTLINE STAFF

Many of Our Library Users Do Not Use Social Networking and Aren't 2.0 Savvy

It's easy to make general statements about our users and what they like or don't like. We base these assumptions on our day-to-day contact with patrons who approach our information desks, email us through chat reference, or call to seek help or advice or to place holds on items for them. However, despite the many physical visitors we have enter through our library doors every day, there are even more visitors accessing our services via our website and library catalogue. More than that, there is an entire community of Web-savvy technology users who don't use our services. In that regard, it is my philosophy to add a "yet" to the end of that statement: "There is an entire community of Web-savvy, technology users who don't use our services—yet."

We focus many of our programming, marketing, and collection on our existing users and the identified needs of those users. For example, we are often creating programs and addressing the needs of our multicultural community, services to children and older adults, and the disenfranchised. However, we also make assumptions about these groups and our "silent" patrons. For example, as our communities grow and reflect a larger population of retired individuals, an argument is often made that our seniors have no need for or interest in the ability to share and create content within a catalogue because they have no skills or interest in that area. However, in a 2009 Nielson report, we can see that the use of the Internet among seniors has seen an increase of over 55 percent in the past five years and a 53 percent increase in the past two years in use of social networking and blog sites ("Six Million More Seniors Using the Web Than Five Years Ago," 2009). And, of course, there is the unrepresented group of users in the library, one that often includes the highest group of taxpayers in the community: the 25- to 45-year-old crowd. Working professionals are a key group of social networking and technology-driven individuals that libraries have the ability to access with next generation catalogues. To them, it's about ease of use and the same type of online presence and service they receive from commercial sites. Used to finding information without assistance and wanting to share that information with friends, this group of library nonusers may benefit from what next generation catalogues offer.

The key to addressing professionals who dismiss next generation catalogues as social networking sites or as a product that is too sophisticated for library users is to approach the argument logically and armed with statistics. There is an abundance of research and ongoing statistics that provide significant proof that we do not give our patrons enough credit in their knowledge of technology and its use. As public librarians, we are quick to pass judgment based on our own experiences with our customers rather than the research and evidence available to us.

Suggesting and Recommending Is My Responsibility

Readers' advisory services may be one of the most effected services impacted by the implementation of social catalogues and social features within the catalogue. Often, when seeking to implement social catalogues or unique features that may enhance a sharing and recommended feel to our catalogues, backroom staff are told to "tread lightly." This feeling of having to tread lightly is likely the unfortunate result of a lack of communication and understanding as to how social catalogues influence, enhance, and complement readers' services. Unfortunately, many view it as replacing or removing the need for readers' services and, as a result, readers' advisory staff within the library. Unfortunately, as stated previously, for most of us it is a knee-jerk reaction to be concerned about other services that may or may not influence our own skills and responsibilities.

With readers' services enjoying a growth of popularity and as an area of library services that will likely continue to play a large part in the future of libraries, it is only natural that next generation catalogues, with their social features, incorporate functions that support this service. However, much of the concern and debate arises when cataloguing librarians or librarians working in the back room make decisions to incorporate these features without the direct input of frontline readers' advisors. There are several sides to this concern, and depending on what area of library service you work in, your perspective will differ from another professional's perspective.

In an ideal situation, backroom staff are considered readers' advisors and thought of as the driving force behind remote readers' services within the library. As a result, they are entrusted with making decisions that enhance all readers' services and not viewed as colleagues setting out to replace individual and personal readers' services. Unfortunately, in many libraries where librarians in the back room have not been afforded the RA training that frontline staff have been offered or where a lack of communication between frontline staff and backroom staff is the norm, the readers' services expertise resides among frontline staff only. As a result, frontline staff often view the role of adopting a social catalogue as anything more than a "traditional" catalogue as a threat or, at the very least, as an invasion of their services and expertise. That's unfortunate as many librarians who work in the back room are knowledgeable in their own right when it comes to remote access, the needs of patrons who use the catalogue, and the tools that will make the library catalogue more useful and intuitive for staff and patrons. As a result, concern and fear are standing in the way of strong and beneficial collaborative relationships and opportunities that can only enhance our services.

The real misunderstanding may arise from many of the points raised in this book, such as a lack of communication, a feeling of ownership of a specific service, and a suspicion of new technologies. Next generation catalogues do not replace frontline staff or their expertise.

Suggesting and recommending books isn't just about what staff have to offer and personal contact through a one-on-one RA conversation. Like many changes that have occurred in libraries, we are used to the traditional service model where we, the librarians, recommend books and patrons listen to our suggestions. While trained readers' advisors bring with them a tool-box of skills that cannot be replaced by reader to reader interaction, many readers want just that—a way to share with other readers and not to interact with staff. Other readers are more comfortable sharing reading suggestions in a more removed setting, and social catalogues offer opportunities for those readers. It is a new opportunity for staff to take advantage of what next generation catalogues offer so that they can bring their RA skills into the catalogue, assist readers in making contact with each other, and pro-mote an environment where conversations about books and the appeal of books happen.

CATALOGUING STAFF

The Catalogue Needs to Be Where the Users Are

The idea that the catalogue is a dying resource is a common statement made by cataloguing staff and frontline staff. In fact, in November 2010, Karen Schneider, director of the Cushing Library at Holy Names University in Oakland, California, tweeted that "the local catalog is one user service, but proportionately, it is just a small (and shrinking) component of our svcs" (Schneider 2010). Other professionals agree that while the catalogue is useful, it needs to become a resource that can be broken apart, sharing metadata in a variety of ways rather than maintaining the data in a boxlike compartment, not easily shared and restricted in its use.

While I agree in the latter statement—that we need to explore the uses of the information contained within our bibliographic records—I think it unfair to judge the current next generation catalogue by its limitations based on what may be possible in future versions of these catalogues. Just as we buy in to the current generation of smartphones, taking for granted their immense improvement over the cell phones from three to five years ago, so we look at our next generation catalogues. Rather than commenting on how far we've come, we are still echoing the popular phrase that "we need to be where the users are."

Many next generation catalogues allow for sharing information in Face-book, through email, and through a variety of social media sites. Even libra-ries without social catalogues have embraced a feeling of being "out there." They have done this by creating library catalogue search widgets for iGoogle users to place on their home pages or a widget for placement on Facebook's user profile page that allows immediate searching of their local catalogues. Others are creating applications for mobile phones so that the library and its services are right at a user's fingertips.

When viewing this statement, "we need to be where the users are," and the possibilities of how to respond, it's important to consider the following factors. If your library has the resources to create widgets for users to place on their iGoogle pages and Facebook profiles or the budget to have these widgets or a mobile application created for the library, it is not surprising that staff may hesitate to invest in a next generation catalogue. As is the case when we consider how best to offer a service, there are many perspectives on what is best for the library catalogue and how we are to proceed with the catalogue in the future. However, a new group of backroom librarians are exploring the possibility that it isn't enough just to be "out there" where the users are and are providing options for the users based on how they want to manipulate the information in our library catalogue. This may mean being able to create a search that extracts all of the records on Salvador Dali's life and manipulating the results to provide a printable bibliography or measuring how many volumes of Shakespeare the library has in its collection compared to Jane Austen.

Defining among your staff and decision makers what it means to be "out there" and how the catalogue can answer that need is the key to addressing concerns regarding where our catalogue should be and how we want it to be used. Some may opt for a more traditional approach, while others look at next generation catalogues as the first step into not only being where the users are but also understanding that these catalogue may finally allow the breaking apart of bibliographic information so that it becomes more than a discovery tool and a true data-mining source.

Get Rid of the Catalogue and the Website and Dump Everything into a Single Source? Ridiculous!

This is often a statement made by cataloguers who do not understand the technical functions of a next generation catalogue. It's easy to make assumptions that the only way to include additional data sources in a catalogue is by "dumping" all of the data into it, thereby rendering the entire catalogue useless and full of errors, lacking uniformity, and having irretrievable information. For cataloguers who pride themselves on creating high-quality bibliographic data, they worry about the integrity of that data being compromised with the introduction of additional data sources. Others make this statement to create panic among their colleagues, creating a diversion from their own fears and apprehensions, all the while attempting to create the same fear among their peers. I've seen this on popular listservs within the profession, and it never fails to bring forth a variety of concerns, tempered by professionals who have experience or an understanding not just in the cataloguing side of the profession but the technical side as well.

Many of the discovery tool overlays, which are the most popular forms of next generation catalogues presently seen in public libraries, are able pull information from a variety of data sources. As a result, when searching the catalogue, you may also retrieve results about community events, programs being offered by the library, library hours, and even information and links to local museum collections. This information does not become part of our bibliographic database but rather is an identified source of information that has been deemed useful, and through data identification and mining, the information is extracted. As a result, it is displayed within the catalogue in a manner that reflects how our bibliographic records appear. Santa Cruz Public Library provides a very good example of this. Using the discovery tool AquaBrowser, the library pulls in information from the catalogue (bibliographic database), the library website, a community information database, a newspaper clipping file, and a local news index. While all of the results display uniformly, all are not part of the bibliographic database, and therefore it's not a "dumping ground" for a variety of information. Rather, it is an organized data-mining search engine that highlights local results and needs without interfering with the integrity of any of the data sources.

CONCLUSION

It is only natural that with the emergence of new technologies and the "mashing up" of library services, apprehension, debate, and legitimate positions for and against these changes will arise. In the past, much of the "mashing up" has been done on the frontline staff side of library services. Exploring the opportunities that external databases offer as a resource outside of the catalogue, as well as links to websites and the use of uncatalogued books to increase circulation, are all ways in which this has occurred. In addition, frontline staff have been the primary providers of instructional classes on how to use the catalogue as well as advocates to advise cataloguers of errors in the catalogue and suggestions for reclassifying and recataloguing items. While it can be argued that many of those responsibilities should fall to cataloguing staff, it has been a position many of us have accepted. In fact, faced with the continuous threat of outsourcing in years past, cataloguers were often too busy to focus on anything but output and the quality of bibliographic records they were providing to justify their positions.

As a result, when viewing the many arguments for and against next generation catalogues, it is interesting to see not only the similarities but also the difference in frontline and backroom staff positions. While both sides of public service—frontline and backroom—are worried about the impact on their expertise and skills, frontline staff view any additional uses of the catalogue beyond that of the traditional model as their responsibility and an infringement on their expertise where backroom staff should tread lightly. However, backroom staff are still caught up in providing a high-quality product that reflects on a justification for their existence.

Next generation catalogues will not be successful if frontline staff and backroom staff continue to work separately in their respective silos.

Cataloguers can provide exceptional bibliographic records, and vendors can provide intuitive interfaces and a variety of interesting and possibly service-altering functions, but without buy-in, support, and understanding from frontline public services staff, even the most efficient, in-depth, and intuitive library catalogue will fail.

Why is this? While social catalogues remain in their infancy, many feature-rich and impressive catalogues have been implemented and, ultimately, will fail in the eyes of the public and staff because frontline staff don't bother to learn about them. However, frontline staff can be only partially blamed for not learning about them. Cataloguers need to take a proactive approach in teaching and promoting the usefulness and collaborative benefits of our future catalogues. But it's not as easy as saying, "Let's hold a meeting, show some PowerPoints, and start collaborating." While in some libraries this may work, most of us have to deal with committees, approvals, and juggling other projects and services that are equally important to sustain and promote. Librarians are known to wear many hats in the course of a day, and these multiple duties make it difficult for cataloguers to create a unique and persuasive enough argument for frontline staff to step away from their own in-branch responsibilities and take the time to inform themselves about a new library catalogue. As evidence of this, very few frontline staff at present are aware of what a social catalogue is and how it can benefit their own responsibilities and services. I'm aware of one library that beta launched a social catalogue and, a year later, still had managers and branch staff questioning how to use the most basic functions. This is not a unique situation. If branch staff don't know how to use our new catalogues, how will they promote these same features and its benefits to patrons? And, without understanding the rich features and potential of next generation catalogues, how can we enrich and enhance all of our services for patrons, which is the goal we all share?

REFERENCES

"Nice Step toward What a Catalog Can Become." *AUTOCAT*, June 2011. Available online at http://comments.gmane.org/gmane.education.libraries.autocat/40016 (accessed June 29, 2011).

Schneider, Karen. Twitter feed. November 4, 2010.

"Six Million More Seniors Using the Web Than Five Years Ago." *Nielson Wire*, December 10, 2009. Available online at http://blog.nielsen.com/nielsenwire/online_mobile/six-million-more-seniors-using-the-web-than-five-years-ago (accessed December 12, 2010).

CHAPTER 4

Readers' Services and the Catalogue

When first writing about readers' services and the catalogue, I included readers' advisory services in Chapter 5 as a traditional, core library service. However, readers' services within public libraries are facing a similar pivotal "coming of age" as that of the catalogue. Because of this, I decided to devote an entire chapter to the budding relationship that RA services and social catalogues are currently enjoying and can build on within the public library framework.

In the past, readers' advisory services was limited to librarians recommending books based on their opinions as to what constituted "good" reading. As many of you can imagine, Harlequin romance novels rarely made the cut! In fact, leisure reading of popular fiction was often judged as elementary or "lowbrow." Instead, readers were provided with classics such as *A Tale of Two Cities*, *Pride and Prejudice*, or *Tom Sawyer*. To most of us, that type of recommending appears antiquated and silly. However, there are practicing professionals who remember those days and many of you who might have experienced these types of recommendations prior to becoming librarians or library professionals. Today, this practice might even still be found within the walls of current public libraries, another similarity to the traditional thinking on the role of library catalogues. However, like the library catalogue and its ability to take on a new and expanding role within libraries, readers' advisory services is also repositioning itself with public libraries to become a core service and one enjoying increasing popularity among patrons.

READERS' ADVISORY SERVICES

For most of us, our current readers' advisory models are heavily based on our traditional reference interview structure. It starts with a roving RA approaching a reader in the library or a patron approaching an RA staff member, striking up a conversation about books that gradually leads to reading suggestions and recommended titles. This model works. We've enhanced it, adding additional tools to aid our rovers (such as laptops), and provided training to our staff that makes the readers' experience even better. The advocates who have shaped the RA interview, the training, the literature, and the art of how we go about offering reading suggestions and understanding readers have turned RA into the thriving, popular, and ever-growing service it is today. As such, it is hard to convey the message that social software and, more specifically, social catalogues do not replace the expertise of RAs, but they do increase our resources and take advantage of the expertise found throughout our library system and our community.

It is important to critically examine how our services are meeting the needs of our users in this social environment. Are we meeting our readers' needs? How have our readers' needs changes from the start of our services? What are our strengths and weaknesses?

In his 2006 article "Improving the Model for Interactive Readers' Advisory Services," Neil Hollands examines the assumptions that many of us make about the traditional RA model we've come to rely on as the foundation of RA services. In an attempt to rethink how readers' services are offered in libraries, Hollands explores six assumptions that we make about our traditional model:

1. That readers initiate or approach an RA with reading questions
2. That the staff member approached will have the knowledge to answer the RA questions
3. That through our RA interviews, we gather enough information to provide good RA services
4. That time constraints do not interfere with the quality of RA services that we provide
5. That the use of databases and other RA sources are easy to use while conducting face-to-face RA interviews
6. That we sufficiently document our RA discussions so that they lead to successful follow-up (Hollands 2006)

When Hollands wrote this article, it was in the context of promoting Williamsburg Regional Library's reading suggestion service called "Looking for a Good Book" in Williamsburg, Virginia. Rather than a face-to-face RA interview, a reading preference form was made available to patrons. As an alternative to the standard impromptu RA interview, the documentation that was collected through these reading preference forms and built on allowed Williamsburg to provide quality readers' services to a greater number of patrons while fitting in with the realities of daily practice (Hollands 2006). Hollands's article and ideas will be explored in greater depth later in this chapter by Duncan Smith in his contributing essay "Channelling RA."

The success of this service as an extension beyond the traditional RA model is proof that we can and should explore new ways to reach patrons. It also demonstrates how new and innovative avenues of RA services can benefit and enhance both our readers' and our RA services to the community.

But why should we explore the library catalogue rather than the website or some other software to enhance RA services? At the end of the day, readers' advisors and patrons come back to the catalogue to find the book for the reader. If the collection is vital to libraries, whether it is in electronic or paper format, than we need to focus on the fact that, in the end, our services revolve around what is found in the catalogue. It is common to hear a readers' advisors admit that after finding a handful of reading suggestions in an outside RA resource, they are discouraged when they return to the library catalogue to find the titles already checked out, with a large list of holds, or that they are not part of the collection.

When readers do decide to go to our online e-branches, many remote readers don't think to look anywhere but the library catalogue. It is the natural tool that readers turn to when they are looking for something to read from the library because that's where the collection is. However, this is often preceded by a visit to Amazon or some other outside source that provides reading recommendations, read-alikes, or "users who have bought [read] 'X' also bought [read] 'Y.'" But if library catalogues include read-alike titles, user and staff reviews, or appeals terminology in bibliographic records, we have an advantage over these outside sources. Rather than generating recommended titles based on algorithms and subject key words, our lists would be based on the collective expertise of readers' advisors, local statistics, and similar appeal elements. While readers aren't experiencing a face-to-face RA interview, they are using our expertise to find themselves a book through our enriched, personalized content.

Many libraries have already taken advantage of social software and technologies to enhance readers' advisory services. This confirms that there is an awareness among RAs that it is necessary to reach out to readers, even in a service that has traditional been offered in-house. But what has been missing and continues to be neglected by many libraries is the interaction with the community.

Readers' advisors are using a variety of software to reach readers. These include RSS feeds, Twitter, RA blogs, RA pages, and Facebook groups. We're asking our readers to follow us, read what we are suggesting, and explore a variety of books they may never have considered. But let's examine what we're doing with these supposedly "social" technologies or at least how we're using them.

Blogs may be the best example for us to examine. How many readers' services teams maintain blogs in their libraries? What type of interaction do they have with their reading community? Do our readers contribute comments to our blogs? Do they offer reading suggestions or reading experiences? In the end, whose reading suggestions are we offering when we write our blog posts? Based on whose preferences? Or are we simply thinking of topics that are timely and trying to create a list of recommended reads? While blog hits may be high and statistics impressive, if we're not inviting our readers to contribute, we've just lost that face-to-face discussion that is the foundation of the interactive readers' advisory service. We've also neglected to take advantage of the opportunity to collect documentation on readers' thoughts or the ideas of our larger reading community that allows us to follow-up with reading suggestions.

It is important to note that while we should not minimize the importance of our blogs, we do need to think about the online environment in which we are operating. We are steeped in a society that expects to interact, recommend, and share. But are we allowing our readers to share? Are we capturing the readers' reading experiences that we value so much? Are we providing a space where they feel invited to share those experiences on our blogs? Or are we taking advantage of the trust that we have created within the branch and assuming that it carries over into our blogs, Facebook pages, and tweets? When we perform our in-house, face-to-face RA interviews, we emphasize the need to listen to what our readers are saying and how to ask the right questions to assist them in finding books. But this has not yet been demonstrated by our use of online social software.

While it's easy to point to the deficiencies in the library catalogue and cataloguing practices to address why we haven't turned to them for solutions to remote access, it has to be acknowledged that both have evolved, expanded, and advanced more in the past 20 years than many of our other core library services. We've moved from a paper inventory of our collections to an online electronic inventory and now to an interactive, more patron-focused and interactive patron-driven catalogue that includes user-generated and RA-driven content. This means that while in the past the library catalogue may not have been very helpful to readers' services, the same might not be said for the catalogue of today—and, it is hoped, not for the library catalogues of tomorrow. While card catalogues had simple access points, such as title, author, and subject, the content of bibliographic records today holds a wealth of information that continues to expand. The ability to work with cataloguers to enhance these records further is available to all of us, whether our records are provided by vendors or originate locally from our cataloguing departments.

Social catalogues are library catalogues that encourage interaction and contribution by users. They allow for user-generated ratings, tags, and reading lists as well as reviews written by readers. Given that patrons have been trying to add content to our catalogues for years (think of the penciled-in notes made by readers even in our card catalogues), we are finally inviting them to contribute and assist us in enhancing their library. As a result, the idea of a "social" library catalogue should be as exciting to RAs as it is to cataloguers. Rather than providing content generated exclusively by library professionals, we are asking our readers to add content. This mirrors the shift in frontline public service from that of "telling" readers what is good for them to listening to their reading interests and needs. What are their reading preferences? What type of material is a certain branch reading? What type of books are they recommending to friends? This is the future of the library catalogue: a new, interactive and collaborative catalogue that is only in its infancy. As a result, next generation library catalogues have the ability to create strong, RA-driven public libraries.

Once again, it is important to stress that many professionals are concerned that social catalogues are trying to create another social networking site. This creates visions of the library catalogue becoming another Facebook, LibraryThing, or even Twitter. Chapter 3 examined this hesitation as well as many other arguments for and against social catalogues. The real hesitation, perhaps, for concluding that social catalogues are another social networking site can be attributed to the term "social." Perhaps these new catalogues should be more appropriately called collaborative or interactive library catalogues. In the end, they are simply the next generation of library catalogues and, in the users' mind, will continue to be called the name by which they are most familiar. This could be the information portal, library catalogue, online card catalogue, online public access catalogue (OPAC), and so on. Whatever the name, it is the collaborative, interactive, and sharing aspect that should be explored. Collecting statistics, reading the reviews our readers are writing, and viewing reading lists created by our community will help us create documentation on books and appeals that we can use to enhance our readers' advisory services. This will allow us to collect data based on all of our readers' needs and not just those who approach our RAs within the branches. As a result, our community will assist in shaping our book displays and impact our choice of appeal elements, author readings, programs, and, ultimately, collections.

Using the information gleaned from user generated content is similar to when we listen in on readers' conversations in the park, in the mall, on the bus, or at other locations outside of the library. It allows us to identify books that are popular and widely read within our communities. It also allows us a glimpse into how our readers are using appeals terminology and how they are relating one book to another.

The user-generated content in social catalogues is what is often referred to as folksonomies. Folksonomies reflect the users' vocabulary and accommodate new concepts and trends that may or may not be in our RA vocabulary. In the end, what results is an indication of our community's desire lines—which are the expressions of the direct needs of our users (Spiteri 2006, 1–2).

These desire lines are important to readers' advisors for several reasons:

- They reflect the needs and interests of the community and, in particular, their reading desires and needs.
- They create an online community of users with the same interests based on tagging patterns, similar reviews, and reading lists.
- It allows library staff to build collections on what users want and are using, including indicating to RAs what books are popular within a community and why (Spiteri 2006, 1–2).

This understanding of our community, such as asking what our readers are reading, exploring their reading appeals, and what type of adjectives they are using to express those appeals, bears a direct correlation into what RA leaders such as Joyce Saricks, Neal Wyatt, and Duncan Smith advocate.

The use of information that can be observed and mined by social catalogues gives us more time to think about reading suggestions and provides yet another venue to bring readers' services to the users rather than asking our readers to come to our physical branches.

In Neal Wyatt's 2007 article "2.0 for Readers," she writes that "the entire point of RA is to reach readers" (Wyatt 2007). In fact, Wyatt suggests that the core of readers' advisory services is built on conversations with the reader that allow us to "adapt, retool, and refine additional suggestions" based on "frequent, if not constant, evaluation and use of reader input" (Wyatt 2007).

By encouraging the use of social technology to enhance readers' services, Wyatt believes that RA work will be strengthened because it will "deepen and broaden the interaction, introduce new ways of connecting books to other items, and enable librarians to enlist the entire community of readers in the collaborative creation of RA services for everyone" (Wyatt 2007).

While Wyatt was talking specifically about 2.0 technologies, social catalogues, as one of the primary faces of our library to remote users, combines all of the interactive, collaborative opportunities that 2.0 offers, but it centers on our collections. As a result, it is a highly valuable tool to RAs given that remote users looking for a good book will be heading directly into the library catalogue to find it. Accordingly, that's where readers' advisors want to be too. In fact, it is not only librarians and RA experts who are recognizing the potential role that next generation catalogues are playing in readers' services.

Whether your library uses enriched content from LibraryThing, Serials Solutions, or NoveList, vendors are recognizing the importance of including elements of RA services in the catalogue. Many of us are familiar with the now standard use of enriched content, which often includes cover art, access to the table of contents, and searching inside the book. However, vendors are exploring additional ways in which to enhance catalogues beyond that of standard enriched content and even beyond the user-generated content that includes tagging and creating reading lists.

NoveList

NoveList, recognized as a leading vendor in the readers' advisory field, has created a product that inserts recommended titles into the bibliographic records of the library catalogue. Extracting the information from the NoveList database, NoveList Select compares your library holdings against the existing read-alikes and recommended titles in the database. Rather than recommending a book the library doesn't own, NoveList Select will display only suggested reading titles based on the holdings in your library's collection.

Recognizing that this is the first product to do this based on documentation and reading preferences and built and created by professionals rather than algorithms, it can be concluded that other vendors will be following NoveList's lead and finding similar ways to extract external database information for insertion into bibliographic records in the catalogue. This acknowledgment that library catalogues play a central role in RA services reinforces the fact that vendors are recognizing the ever-increasing role and importance library catalogues are playing in all areas of library service. Vendors may even be recognizing our catalogues' potential before us, understanding that they are not just "static inventories," separate and apart from our other services, but rather an integral tool for delivering our services to users.

NoveList also includes appeals terminology in their catalogued book records. Rather than simply applying subject headings, the cataloguers created and defined a list of authority appeals terminology to be applied to books within their database in collaboration with RA appeals experts.

This appeals terminology differs from subject headings because it attempts to apply descriptive terms that capture the readers' experiences. The appeals terms are defined under four broad appeals categories: pace, story line, tone, and writing style. Adding these elements into our library catalogues should also be considered and should not be summarily dismissed because authorities for this terminology are not standardized by a national library. Standardization will develop over time.

The NoveList database is a database: a catalogue. To implement these kinds of innovative ideas into the library catalogue for users to benefit from is possible in next generation catalogues as well as our existing, legacy catalogues. Doing this requires cataloguers to work closely with readers' advisors and, in fact, reinforces the need for becoming readers' advisors so that they, too, obtain a level of understanding and expertise that will allow for appeals to be created and implemented into cataloguing practices and, ultimately, into our bibliographic records.

LIBRARYTHING

Recognized by librarians as a strong reading tool and often used as a comparison for our library catalogues, LibraryThing has also acknowledged the importance of RA services within their database. In early 2010, they launched a beta version for a new type of recommendations: Read Alikes. According to LibraryThing's blog, "The 'Read Alikes' recommendations supplement our existing automatic and members recommendations. 'Read Alikes' are based directly on the members who have your books—the people who 'read alike' you" ("Beta," 2010).

In 2011, based on a user's suggestion, LibraryThing took their recommendations feature a step further. The user wrote to Tim Spalding suggesting that the ability to "get a list of books from a friend's library that are recommended for me based on my library" would be a great feature ("New Recommendations," 2011). An excellent idea, LibraryThing listened to its user and implemented the idea.

These are types of social interactivities and conversations that readers want with each other. Many users want to access friends' libraries, while others are interested in anonymity and simply want to find additional recommendations or read-alikes from other community members or patrons. The demand for features such as this do exist, which is why we are seeing them appear with increasing frequency in external databases and tools. Our library catalogues—our new *social* catalogues—need to find a way to create these features to offer them to our users. If we cannot offer them, we need to be able to integrate these outside services into our catalogues so that patrons are not forced to visit a variety of sites to perform simple functions—to find other users with similar reading interests, to share reading interests, to find reading suggestions, and to place holds on these items. It should not be necessary to visit multiple sites or to visit the library personally for a one-on-one conversation with a readers' advisor to perform these tasks. This is where social catalogues, as an extension of the physical, social space of public libraries, come into play. Many next generation catalogues are starting to offer features that assist in readers' services or at least provide a foundation we can begin to build on to provide RA within the catalogue. The direction these social catalogues take will be shaped by many of us. If we recognize the strong relationship between readers' services and social catalogues, we can play a role in the development of the features that we require to make it work. Even without acquiring a social catalogue, we can often take steps within our existing library practices to enhance the role library catalogues play in readers' services. In Chapter 3, the case was made for building a relationship between cataloguers and readers' advisors. Chapter 6 explores ways of integrating readers' services features into our existing legacy catalogues.

RA SERVICES AND A NEW MODEL
FOR A SOCIAL CATALOGUE

What would happen if vendors of readers' advisory databases decided to challenge and compete with the library catalogue's role in libraries? Perhaps they consider replacing it completely with their own products? While arguments can be made that readers' advisory databases do not have the depth of content or the records for each holding of every library, let's suppose that public libraries begin focussing their collections primarily on leisure reading. Is our next social catalogue not a catalogue at all but a database that has already created the links and relationships among reading materials that library catalogues are attempting to provide? Readers' services databases can provide read-alikes, appeals terminology, subgenres, and often protagonists' names and ages. This type of rich content, lacking in the majority of bibliographic records within our existing catalogues, is rich in detail and provides a wealth of access points and "bookmarking," or tagging of terms, that is extremely beneficial to readers and readers' advisors. With printable reading lists, cover art, tagging features, and strong searching capabilities, it might be readers' services databases that become the primary library catalogue for public libraries. If vendors decide to focus on interoperability between integrated library systems and databases, these vendors might be providing the new social catalogues to libraries. If we can imagine a future where our next generation library catalogues are born out of readers' advisory databases, we can also imagine these catalogues offering the same key characteristics that readers' services rely on—relationships, conversations, constant feedback, and listening to our readers. As a result, conversations, community, and a social space become key characteristics of our future library catalogues.

Perhaps, to fully understand the role library catalogues can play in readers' services, we can look to practicing readers' advisors for their views on the future of readers' advisory. In that regard, the following essay by Duncan Smith provides insight into the current state of readers' advisory services and the role that online interaction and social catalogues play in the future of this service. Specifically, note the need for access to remote services and the ability for readers to access RA services outside the physical walls of the library. In that regard, after reading Smith's thoughts and considering the content provided throughout this chapter, you, the professional, should have a greater appreciation of how and why our future library catalogues play an integral role in readers' services.

Channelling RA by Duncan Smith

RA AS A TRANSFORMATIVE ACT

Sometimes there is a magical quality to readers' advisory, like when you are talking with a reader and their reading interests and yours overlap. A personal example involves my working with a reader who enjoyed Amy Tan's *The Joy Luck Club*. This reader enjoyed the fact that this was a book about mother-daughter relationships and about people from a culture that was different from hers. She liked the fact that the book left her feeling hopeful and because she was busy and frequently tired when she read—she appreciated *The Joy Luck Club*'s episodic or vignette-like structure (it started out as a short story collection after all).

As she finished telling me about her reading experience and what she remembered about the book, she looked at me, sighed, and said, "It's not going to be easy to find another book like that." After a little thinking and some searching, I suggested Alvarez's *How the Garcia Girls Lost Their Accents*, Naylor's *The Women of Brewster Place*, Whitney's *How to Make an American Quilt*, Smith's *Fair and Tender Ladies*, and Tyler's *Dinner at the Homesick Restaurant*. My reader thought that the Alvarez title sounded interesting. She had heard of *The Women of Brewster Place* and Whitney's *How to Make an American Quilt*. Luckily for me, she had read Tyler's book, and it was one of her favorites. And right before she exclaimed, "I'll take them all, I want to read them all," she said, "I see what all of these books have in common. They are stories about women."

And that's the magical part! The magic is not that I (or we) through our personal reading or our expertise with resources find other books for our readers. The aspect of this interaction that is alchemical, that is transformative, is when our conversation about the reader's interests results in a change in the reader, a new awareness that the books she likes have something in common and especially how these titles relate to her newly discovered awareness of her reading.

As librarians, we also know how rare and precious these transactions are because for everyone of them, there are many others that result not in the golden afterglow of success but the leaden thud of failure. Writing in 1996, Kenneth Shearer found than even though Joyce Saricks had been urging librarians to begin readers' advisory transactions by asking the reader about their reading experience since 1989, this information was solicited in only 24 percent of the 53 readers' advisory cases contained in his study of North Carolina public libraries (Shearer 1996, 17). In an article published in *Library Journal* in 2000, Anne May and her coauthors found that in the suburban libraries they visited around New York City, "a non-methodical, informal, and serendipitous response was the norm to a patron's request for a 'good read'" (May et al. 2000, 40–44).

Readers' advisory service has improved since the early Shearer and May studies and RA practice is becoming less nonmethodical and informal if you consider the use of resources as evidence of the professionalization of this important aspect of our practice. In a forthcoming article, Catherine Sheldrick Ross and others summarize the results of an eight-year-long study involving 641 cases similar to Shearer's and May's (Ross, in press). In the first year of this study of libraries in Ontario, 50 percent of respondents did not consult any resource. By 2010, the number had declined to 27 percent. Over the course of this study, there is a steady increase in the integration of standard library resources into the RA transaction. For example, use of NoveList and NoveList Plus in these cases went from 0 percent in 2002 to 28 percent of cases throughout the course of the study. Of particular interest is the use of the catalogue in these transactions. Over the course of this study, the library catalogue is the second most consulted resource being used in 25 percent of cases. An additional item of interest in this study is the trend in types of resources used over the course of the study. While in the overall study, NoveList resources were the most often consulted, in the 2010 data, NoveList was consulted in 29 cases, while the catalogue was consulted in 37 cases and the library website in 29 cases. The increasing use of library catalogues and websites may be the result of the increasing presence of readers' advisory–related content in these resources.

In essence, what we have here is a distribution issue. Delivering readers' advisory service from desks frequently results in mismatches between a reader's interests and a staff member's knowledge or expertise. This delivery strategy is unfortunate in that it results in the reader not having the library's best resources at their disposal when they come to our desks looking for a good book to read. Here's another illustration from my years at the circulation desk.

When I was working at the Forsyth County (North Carolina) Public Library's Kernersville branch, a woman came in who loved Regency Romances. While I was able to find a few titles for her, I also knew that our head of business reference down at the Main Library was a Regency fan. In fact, she had a deal with cataloguing where she got all of the new Regencies first! So while I was able to provide my reader with a few possibly interesting titles, what really ramped up her enthusiasm was when I got Joy (our head of business reference) on the phone and they spent the next five minutes talking about the authors they both liked. This also resulted in the reader going back to the stacks and checking out several more titles. This tale had a happy ending because I happened to remember Joy's reading interests, but in these days and times of tight budgets and increasing demands for accountability, can we afford to underutilize the knowledge and expertise of any of our staff, especially since for every dollar we spend on the books and materials that our readers are coming to us for, we spend $4.76 on staff (American Library Association 2009, 8)? Addressing this mismatch by developing strategies that more effectively match readers and staff expertise at the desk would result in much-improved readers' advisory service for those readers who know that the library is a place where you can seek help in finding your next book to read. However, we know that only a few of our readers actually come to our desks seeking this type of service. This knowledge isn't just limited to anecdotal evidence.

Where Are All the Readers?

In *From Awareness to Funding*, the Online Computer Library Center (2008) funded a study that looked at a variety of issues around library use and willingness to vote for increased library support. One aspect of this study was to analyze both library and nonlibrary users and to group these into market segments. One segment was the "Super Supporters." This market segment contains the largest percentage of voters who would definitely vote for increased library funding. This group uses a wide range of library resources and services, including borrowing nonfiction and best-selling titles; they use the library to research or learn more about hobbies; they access the library's online resources; and they get recommendations from librarians about books (especially kids' books). In addition to being voracious readers, this group also shares several attitudes about the library and about librarians. For example, this group recognizes the librarian's superior research skills, believes that librarians are more than researchers (they are passionate advocates for the library), have deep emotional connections to the library, and believe that the library transforms lives—including their own.

Eighty percent of this market segment would definitely vote in favor of a library referendum, and while they are self-described voracious readers, they are not the market segment that makes the heaviest use of our collections. That distinction belongs to the "Just for Fun" segment. While this segment represents only 7.1 percent of all survey respondents, its accounts for 23.9 percent of all library visits. They are heavy consumers of books, magazines, newspapers, videos, and DVDs. They are very knowledgeable about the services that the library offers, but they lack the emotional connection to the library that the "Super Supporters" have and do not view it as a place of transformation. What is also missing from this segment's profile is any statement about or connection to library staff. What emerges from the description of this group is a user segment that helps themselves to our collections and resources without interacting with library staff. The result is that while this group is knowledgeable about library collections, resources, and services, that knowledge is self-taught. This group evaluates the library based on what they know about our collections and services—without the benefit of staff knowledge and expertise. What is also interesting about this group is that they are heavy users of the online catalogue. While 51 percent of survey respondents indicated that they used the online catalogue, 76 percent of the "Just for Fun" segment use it.

The Changing Nature of Library Visits

From Awareness to Funding sheds some light on why more folks aren't lined up at our desks asking for reading guidance. Another key factor in the low number of readers' advisory requests we receive at our desks is that the nature of a visit to the library has changed for many users. In the past, the search for a book began by actually walking through the library's doors. For an increasing number of library users, that is no longer the case.

The Public Library of Charlotte and Mecklenburg County (North Carolina) serves a population of 910,000. In 2010, readers walked through the library's doors 5,836,636 times (Smith 2010). The library circulated 5,523,719 books. While 5.8 million is a lot of library visits, the library's website had 70,116,144 hits.

For every person who walked through the door, the library's website got 12 hits. A significant portion of both library visits and circulation was undoubtedly driven by readers placing holds on popular titles and then coming to the library to pick them up. During this period, the library had 1,481,252 holds placed on books. Of these, 1,218,636 (82 percent) were placed remotely by readers accessing the library's catalogue from outside the library. These figures paint a picture of library use that is somewhat different from our image of readers coming to the library and roaming our shelves to find something good to read. They show that for an increasingly number of users, the virtual equivalent of our physical shelves is our online catalogue.

This is not just a big library trend. At the Downers Grove (Illinois) Public Library, which serves a population of 48,724, 99,724 (86 percent) of the library's 116,047 holds were placed remotely. At the Williamsburg (Virginia) Regional Library, which serves a population of 75,000, 88 percent of holds were remote (130,495 out of 148,015) (Smith 2010).

We are now faced not only with trying to inform and reach those readers who are in the library about our willingness to help them find a good book to read but also communicating it to a growing number of readers who search our catalogue remotely and come into the library only to pick up the materials that they already know about. The advent of e-books is only going to increase this challenge, making it possible not only to search the library holdings remotely but also to borrow a book (via download) without ever setting foot in a library building. How big an issue is this likely to be? Of the three libraries mentioned above, only one has provided downloadable e-books for any length of time. At the Public Library of Charlotte and Mecklenburg County, e-books account for 10 percent of total book circulation.

When readers come into the physical library, we not only have eager staff standing by to help them find the books they will enjoy. We also use a variety of strategies to help users find books on their own. Many of us separate our collections out by genre or use spine labels to help readers browsing shelves determine whether a book is in a genre that interests them. We also create book displays and put out bookmarks or booklists, and in some cases we also borrow strategies employed by bookstores—shelf talkers being one example. As the definition of a library visit shifts from walking through a library's door to a visit to its website or online catalogue, we need to determine ways to push all of the book and reader knowledge that is resident in our staffs to these increasingly popular channels for experiencing the library.

Before implementing any of these strategies, however, we need to be sure that our users would view this content as helpful and interesting and not noise. Early indications are that our users would view the addition of readers' advisory–related content as a very desirable addition, especially adding it to the online catalogue. In a study of online catalogue users, the Evansville (Indiana) Vanderburg Public Library found that 78 percent of respondents wanted to see reading recommendations in their library's online catalogue and that 72 percent of respondents wanted to see series information (Mangold 2010).

**ONE LIBRARY'S RESPONSE

In 2006, Neil Hollands published "Improving the Model for Interactive Readers' Advisory Service" (Hollands 2006, 205–12). This article explores some of the limitations of the traditional models for delivering readers' advisory services, especially delivering those services from a desk. Hollands not only notes the mismatch between a reader's interest and staff expertise already mentioned in this article but also points out that readers' advisory requests are frequently more like research questions than ready reference questions. Ready reference questions, which generally have definite answers, can be discovered by consulting one or two sources and are quickly addressed are perfect for reference or information desks. Readers' advisory questions, which like complex research questions require a more in-depth interview with the reader, consulting several resources and thought into how the information is presented to the reader are not well suited to the rapid pace of today's library desks.

Hollands, who works at the Williamsburg Regional Library, goes on to describe that library's form-based approach to readers' advisory. In essence, this approach involves the reader completing a form about his or her reading interests. This form is then routed to the staff member whose knowledge and expertise is closest to that of the reader. Away from the desk, without the pressure of having to provide an immediate response, the staff member compiles a list of potential titles and then creates annotations that show the connection between the title and the reader's interest, helping the reader see the connection between these potentially unknown authors and titles and his or her interests. The form is provided in paper for those readers who are in the library, but, more important, it is also available online at the library's website for those users accessing the library through this channel.

Over the past several years, Williamsburg has built on their experience with these forms and adopted a multichannel approach to delivering readers' advisory service. In addition to their online form, the staff also maintains a blog. "Blogging for a Good Book" (http://bfgb.wordpress.com) provides Williamsburg's virtual users with one book selection a day from the library staff. Each entry not only highlights a title contained in the library's collection but also communicates the depth and breadth of book knowledge that is held by the staff of this library. This groundbreaking blog has not gone unnoticed by the profession; it won the American Library Association's Louis Shores-Greenwood Publishing Group Award for book reviewing and other library media in 2009 for "being the future of book reviewing." It also won second place in 2010's Salem Press Library Blog Award in the public library category. Users can also subscribe to the blog and receive entries as emails delivered to their in-box or as an RSS feed. The reviews contained in "Blogging for a Good Book" are also linked to relevant title records in the library's catalogue, providing another channel for staff expertise to be featured.

This library has also upgraded their catalogue with readers' advisory content from sources like NoveList, Chilifresh, and LibraryThing. Using NoveList's Content in the Catalog Service, this library has reading recommendations and series information delivered directly to their catalogue from NoveList. They also have encouraged readers to rate and review titles held in their collection with the rating and review service provided by Chilifresh. Tags and reading suggestions from LibraryThing are also available in Williamsburg's catalogue.

Although by most measures the Williamsburg Regional Library would be placed in the medium- to small-sized category, Barry Trott has assembled an extremely knowledgeable and gifted staff when it comes to readers' advisory expertise. This staff has been responsible for the publication of close to seven books on various genres and readers' advisory topics. What is truly remarkable about this library and its adult services department is that their expertise isn't available only from the reference desk. It is available to this library's users 24/7 through the channels that these users use the most—the library's catalogue and website. While Williamsburg's blog may indeed be the future of book reviewing, their methods for delivering readers' advisory are certainly the future of this essential library service.

OPENING DOORS

Readers' advisory service can be defined as those services that do the following:

1. Help readers understand what they like
2. Assist them in finding more of what they like
3. Deepen their appreciation of their reading
4. Support them in sharing their reading with others

In the past, we have focused on delivering these services from within our library's buildings. Today and tomorrow, the future of these services lies in delivering them where our readers are, and that is in our catalogue and on our website.

Recently, I was visiting a library in California. It is a beautiful facility, well positioned on a rolling hill with lots of windows and views of the Pacific. It was built in the 1990s at a cost of $10 million. Walking through the front doors of this jewel of a facility, the first thing I see is a series of self-check machines. Immediately to the left of these machines is a bookshelf with sets of books with rubber bands around them and a user's last name. It is very convenient for a reader to park, walk into the library, get their books, and leave. They can do this without going further than 15 feet inside this $10 million facility.

While this is undoubtedly a timesaving, valuable, and appreciated service for many users, what these users are missing is the opportunity to learn more about the library's extensive collections; the wealth of programs, services, and events that are available to them; and the depth and breadth of the staff's expertise. Our profession cannot afford for our users to be unaware of all that we can provide for them. We need to ensure that whatever channel our readers use to access us, they are provided not only with opportunities to locate the authors and titles they already know about but also with opportunities that open the world of books to them. Our readers need to see the library as a place of discovery and transformation where they learn about new authors and titles, deepen their understanding and appreciation of their reading, and have opportunities to share their experiences with others. The door to richer reading experiences can no longer require walking through a library's doors. It needs to be available through every pathway used by our readers—including our catalogue.

CONCLUSION

Both readers' services and library catalogues are experiencing a transitional period that allows for a unique relationship to build between the two. While vendors are offering readers' services elements within their databases that may impact what our new social catalogues look like and how they are defined, we must acknowledge that the increasing popularity of RA services, together with the increasing demand of quality remote access, positions library catalogues in a unique place. Rather than using numerous resources, links, or external technologies that serve only to "get in the way" of what we are attempting to achieve, we can identify the essential elements of readers' services and implement them in our catalogues. If we do, we can successfully offer remote RA services to our readers wherever they choose to be. As a result, instead of keeping readers' advisory services as an in-house-only service, library catalogues allow RAs to reach our readers and bring their services out into the community and into the readers' homes.

Duncan Smith's essay further serves to identify that users can benefit from accessing our readers' services remotely. Reading is a personal experience, and Duncan captures it best in his opening lines: "Sometimes there is a magical quality to readers' advisory, like when you are talking with a reader and their reading interests and yours overlap." With next generation catalogues, it should be possible to connect with these readers and with readers' advisors who help introduce readers to each other. Rather than walking through our physical library doors, we should be using our library catalogues as online gateways that introduce a world of reading and books wherever our readers are located. With the increasing evidence that readers are accessing our services outside the physical walls of our libraries and, as a result, not always taking advantage of our in-house readers' advisory services and expertise, we need to seek ways to bring our services to our readers. Next generation catalogues are a strong candidate for doing this.

REFERENCES

American Library Association. *The State of America's Libraries*. Chicago: American Library Association, 2009.

"Beta: Read-Alike Recommendations." LibraryThing Blog (March 1, 2010). Available online at http://www.librarything.com/blogs/librarything/2010/03/beta-read-alike-recommendations (accessed June 25, 2011).

Hollands, Neil. "Improving the Model for Interactive Readers' Advisory Service. *Reference and User Services Quarterly* 45, no. 3 (Spring 2006): 205–12.

Mangold, Amy. "Evansville Vanderburgh Public Library and NextReads/NoveList: Partners in Public Service." Paper presented at the annual meeting of the American Library Association, Washington, D.C., June 27, 2010.

May, Anne K., et al. "A Look at Readers' Advisory Services." *Library Journal* 125 (September 15, 2000): 40–44.

"New Recommendations: What Should You Borrow?" LibraryThing Blog (June 22, 2011). Available online at http://www.librarything.com/blogs/librarything/2011/06/new-recommendations-what-should-you-borrow (accessed June 25, 2011).

Online Computer Library Center. *From Awareness to Funding: A Study of Library Support in America*. Dublin, OH: Online Computer Library Center, 2008.

Ross, Catherine Sheldrick, et al. "Summary of RA Library Visits: 2002–2010 (in press).

Shearer, Kenneth D. "Readers' Advisory Transaction in Adult Reading." In *Guiding the Reader to the Next Book*. New York: Neal-Schuman, 1996.

Smith, Duncan. "Delivering RA Services to Readers in a Digital Age." *Ebooks: Libraries at the Tipping Point* (Library Journal Webcast, September 29, 2010).

Spiteri, L. F. "The Use of Collaborative Tagging in Public Library Catalogues." *Proceedings of the American Society for Information Science and Technology* 43 (2006): 1–5.

Wyatt, Neal. "2.0 for Readers." *Library Journal* 132 (2007): 18. Available online at http://www.libraryjournal.com/article/CA6495211.html (accessed December 12, 2010).

CHAPTER 5

The Impact of Social Catalogues on Traditional Library Services

Just like the physical library, the library catalogue can provide users with an interactive, social environment based on trust, familiarity, and a sense of belonging. As stated in previous chapters, this does not mean that the library catalogue should become another yet another social networking site. What we need to determine is what makes the library special. While difficult, it is important to examine why patrons continue to use the library despite having a wealth of information sources at their fingertips. What is unique about the library, and why do patrons continue to use our services? Determining our strongest and most valuable assets may lead to unexpected surprises as to what the community truly enjoys about their libraries. Even if we can identify only a handful of these elements, we can move forward in deciding how best to implement them into the catalogue.

Why the catalogue? Whether travelling, at school, or in the comfort of their own home, users are accessing our libraries through the Internet. In fact, when you look at the statistics regarding where holds are placed on items, the average percentage for most libraries indicates that well over 75 percent of holds are placed remotely (Smith 2010). These statistics strengthen the need to determine how to extend to our remote users that special "something" that we offer within our physical walls. This requires a new way of thinking about our services that calls on us to look beyond our traditional service models.

The earlier chapters in this book examine how patrons want to access our services. We know that patrons want more than just what we offer within our branches. They expect to access our services remotely while the quality of those services remains the same. This ease of access can be blamed on

Google, Facebook, or a variety of other social and information tools, but the reality is that our users expect the same online or "remote" service from libraries as they do from any other information or social outlet. The information provided on our websites—including reference, readers', teens', and kids' pages and a variety of links, forms, and now, blogs—is evidence that we, as professionals, are exploring a variety of ways to get our information out to patrons.

With the changing nature of what "personal" service means and the community's view of access to all services remotely, we are and should be examining how social catalogues can be used as the tool by which to offer our services to remote users.

COLLECTION DEVELOPMENT

While selectors and vendors do their best to create a rich and, ultimately, well-rounded collection, if the collection isn't circulating, it isn't successful. Taking the popular patron feature "suggestions for purchase" a step further, user-generated information can provide useful statistics into community interests and needs. Statistics based on user tags, reviews, and reading lists allow libraries to build collections around user interests and borrowing patterns while still maintaining user privacy.

In many libraries, the collection development department is set up in one of three ways. The first is that of a central selector, located at one branch and often situated within the technical services, or information technology, department. Without personal contact with patrons, they base their purchases on the recommendations sent in from other branches, book reviews, and journals as well as suggestions for purchase made by patrons.

A decentralized collection development structure is also popular. This structure provides for a group of selectors, located at different branches, to select for specific collection. A librarian from one branch may select all of the children's nonfiction items for the entire system, while another may be located across town, selecting all of the DVDs for the library.

The final structure that many libraries have been turning to recently is to refer the selecting to a vendor that supplies items based on a larger popularity scale, determined through mass purchasing and distributing practices by publishers and libraries.

With the information mined through user-generated information, new collection development practices can be examined, taking advantage of the statistics and data that their patrons are providing through their interaction with the catalogue. Rather than an autonomous or even a broad view of purchasing where a "one-size-fits-most" model is applied, user-generated information allows selectors to examine data that identifies items that are being rated highly by their community, items recommended from one reader to another, and items that are added to reading lists as favourites, or actively disliked by patrons. As a result, Spiteri's theory of folksonomies and their ability to form desire lines reflecting the needs and wants of the community can also be applied to collection development practices (Spiteri 2006, 1–2).

Being able to mine data generated by users will provide an overview of the variety of needs found throughout all communities represented by a library system, allowing selectors to examine reading and borrowing practices to create an even stronger and representative collection to the community. Building on readers' advisory services within the catalogue, selectors can turn to their in-house RAs to assist in ordering read-alikes or similar titles based on patterns gleaned from the information generated by catalogues.

In this regard, there is an increasing amount of data that can be mined as social catalogues continue to expand and as the technology behind these catalogues grows. In addition to user-generated information, vendors of next generation catalogues are focussing their efforts on how to manipulate the data for examining numerous functions and usages. This includes isolating borrowing practices for one specific branch in a community as well as determining the items shared with friends through social networking sites.

Taking advantage of the opportunities these data provide to our collection development practices will strengthen a key position many libraries are beginning to take when faced with so many information alternatives: our strengths lie in the personal, local information and resources we provide. Next generation catalogues enhance our current collection development practices beyond our existing models to a level of catering to the needs of our local and diverse community. Just as a readers' advisor knows that it is the experience we are trying to capture and assist our reader in finding, a selector understands that he or she must find not only the blockbuster items—but a diverse and well-rounded collection that suits the needs of and that will be of interest to their diverse communities. User-generated information and the data mined from social catalogues are starting to assist with this and will become an even stronger collection development tool in the future.

YOUTH SERVICES

With the popularity of social networking among teens and tweens, youth services within the library is in an advantageous position to use the social features within next generation catalogues to create an environment where this demographic can utilize these features in a variety of ways.

"What are your friends reading? Want to create your own personal booklist or post your absolute, all-time favourite book to Facebook? Now you can!" Will this grab the attention of your tweens and teens? Maybe, maybe not. But it is important to convey to your younger adults that the catalogue

no longer operates as just an inventory for finding items; it also operates as a tool for sharing, discovering, and creating your own content.

Parents of teen readers have expressed their teens' interest in sharing favourite books through Facebook or seeing what their friends are reading. In fact, what friends are reading is a strong influence on their own reading choices.

We all know how to tag. We find a book, movie, or other item we like and add a tag that's meaningful to us—perhaps a "to read" tag, a "favourites" tag, or a term we feel isn't included in the subject headings but is representative of the item.

What if we asked our teens and tweens to create tags? Perhaps it's a joint effort where teens all use the same tag, such as TEENFAVES, or ask them to jointly create a reading list for a specific topic. For example, what are teens reading on the topic of sex or abuse? How do we do this and have our patrons stay anonymous?

For something that involves tagging their favourite books using the tag TEENFAVES, they would simply use their own user account. Using the TEENFAVES tag, they could search the list as it grows (by their own creation and that of their peers rather than staff). The tag name could be linkable from the teen website, by sharing through social media, or by texting.

Imagine a scenario where there are a handful of teen book clubs throughout several branches. Perhaps each book club has its own user account and there's a competition among the clubs for the best reviews or most interesting reading lists. Engaging our younger library patrons through social software and collaborative projects are ways that social catalogues can promote and enhance youth services.

While some tagging, lists, and reviews are easy to make and can often be lighthearted, a teen who may share his or her user name with friends may still feel uneasy about tagging books about controversial topics. The use of social features within next generation catalogues is a great resource for staff to engage youth in creating reading lists that are relevant to them but perhaps uncomfortable to speak about with staff or each other. By creating a generic user account that can be shared by a group of teens, resource lists and reading lists can be created while maintaining a level of anonymity that will make this group of individuals feel comfortable about sharing these resources.

The user-generated features in social catalogues enable a level of collaboration and sharing not just in a social media sense but also in a community sense where the creators of resources can be made by peers within the community sense with the guidance from staff.

PROGRAMMING

By their very nature, it is relatively easy to accept and acknowledge that social catalogues will impact readers' advisory services and collection development. Not just about discovery or performing a known item search, these catalogues naturally lend themselves to enhancing services that rely on feedback and interaction with the community. As a result, programming is also a service in libraries that can be enhanced through the use of information gleaned from these new catalogues.

We've all experienced programs that were successful within our library. There have also been programs that had great promise or what we, as librarians, believed would be successful but that resulted in low attendance or cancellation.

What makes our programs successful? If we're being honest, it's the amount of community interest that the program has generated or attracted. This can be the result of a successful marketing plan, but, more often than not, it has to do with the topic being related to something timely or of interest to the community. Sometimes it is as simple as the relation to a project at a local school or a celebration in one of the local communities.

In addition to physically reaching out to our communities through visits and meetings, we can often see patterns of interest in our communities by examining searches performed in our catalogues, circulation of specific collections, suggestions for purchase, and reference questions. Beyond these data, which can currently be mined in our current catalogues, next generation catalogues allow us to examine user-generated information in the form of public reading lists, tags, or reviews generated by patrons. Because of this, programming can cater to the interests of the community. In particular, programming focusing around themes that are not as obvious as local events, holidays, or the latest best-sellers have the potential to be identified through use of the information generated by current catalogues as well as next generation catalogues.

However, one of the newest forms of social interaction for programming is reflected in the recording of programs by library staff. When library systems are spread throughout a large geographic area or programs of interest take place during work hours, many patrons are not able to attend. Recently, libraries have been recording programs and linking the recording program with the relevant items within the catalogue. Or, if there is an author reading, catalogues have been providing a link to the recorded program from within the bibliographic record of the author's book.

Here are two examples of how to use next generation catalogues for special events or programming.

Book Clubs

Book clubs are full of individuals who love to discuss books and share opinions. Generally, they tend to be active within the library and, given the right incentive or motivation, make excellent contributors to the social and collaborative side of next generation catalogues.

Imagine the following scenario. There's a keen and active book club at two of your library branches. They are knowledgeable about books and are interested in sharing their opinions on favourite books and what they thought of them. Through the use of social features, these two book clubs can share reading ideas or reading lists or provide an interesting dialogue of book reviews with differing perspectives. Perhaps, using one unique tag, the book clubs can create a list of recommended titles for mystery lovers, romance readers, and so on.

Author Readings/Local Artists/Performers

If an author has come to one of your branches for an author reading and it's been recorded, a link to that reading can be made available in the book's bibliographic record. For example, if you were to visit Halifax Public Libraries' catalogue and search for Alastair MacLeod's title *No Great Mischief*, there is a link to the author's talk and reading. A staff member can easily post this record to Facebook or Twitter or choose among a variety of other ways to share this information. Patrons can too.

With the increasingly popular share function in many next generation catalogues, it is also possible to promote author readings or programs prior to the event. And, if we invite our community to engage in this sharing activity, literary events such as author readings throughout your community can be promoted through the catalogue. For example, imagine a student at a local university finding out about a talk celebrating the anniversary of Harper Lee's book *To Kill a Mockingbird*. A user of the social features in your catalogue, he finds a copy of the book and uploads a link to the record onto Facebook or broadcasts it across Twitter, commenting on a talk, where it's going to be, and when. If he follows your library's Twitter feed, he might include a "mention" of your library (@ZYPublicLib), in turn alerting staff to this talk. This may spark an idea for a display or reading lists or may coincide with a local branch event also celebrating the anniversary.

Social catalogues are not just about obtaining a new catalogue that invites users to collaborate and create information within the catalogue; it's about viewing the catalogue as more than just an inventory that lists the items within a library collection. It's about viewing the library catalogue as a tool that connects patrons with a variety of resources and information in one place rather than on multiple pages on a library website, library blogs, and then again in the catalogue. By taking the position that the library catalogue can be the one portal to all of the library's resources and information, programs occurring within the library should be included within a library catalogue, just as a reading lists are linked into the catalogue, bringing a set of related books or items within the collection.

REFERENCE

We are seeing the idea of the library catalogue as a "local Google" take shape as partnerships with local museums, archives, art galleries, and other community groups are developing with libraries. AquaBrowser, one of the most widely implemented discovery tools in North America, has the ability to search multiple indexes, or databases, within the one search box located in the catalogue. As discussed in a previous chapter, this allows the content in the website, as well as other data sources, to be indexed and searched within the catalogue.

Imagine having a stationary, local database housed at your reference desk. This database is a local, stand-alone database created by the reference staff to include information on all the local artists, musicians, and notable community members mentioned in the library's collection. For example, if your community were in Jamestown, New York, one of the most notable hometown figures would be Lucille Ball. If the reference staff had indexed every item within the collection that mentions or relates to Lucille Ball, it would contain a wealth of information for anyone wishing to research her. If this is done with a variety of community members and figures, both past and present, the only shortcoming is that it is available in-house, on one computer, at your reference desk. In the end, an excellent resource but truthfully, likely not used heavily and rather inconvenient to patrons.

With the cataloguing technology available to us, this entire database can be re-created in MARC format and, if your ILS allows, stored in an additional index or database that sits beside your bibliographic database. Through the use of social catalogues and a single search box, this local database can also be searched, just like the bibliographic database that contains the library's collection. In fact, given the faceted navigation ability of social catalogues, a user who searched for Lucille Ball would be able to narrow their search by choosing which database they would like to pull results from. Perhaps they want to eliminate all databases except for the library catalogue. However, they may want to find local content on Lucille Ball from the reference database or even isolate the programs or community events related to her through the content on the website. Whatever their preference, social catalogues are quickly becoming the primary clearinghouse for these searches and the management of large amounts of information.

With the ability to integrate federated searching into catalogues—which is the searching of subscription databases—reference staff have efficiently decreased the amount of toggling and data sources needed to perform a successful reference interview. When helping patrons, they will also be able to demonstrate a single search in one location rather than navigating the patron first through the library website and subscription database pages and then back to the catalogue. Although found in many legacy catalogues, often one of the most exciting features of next generation catalogues is the live reference chat that can be placed within the catalogue. However, this is more often than not due to the implementation of a simple widget that was placed there by a library's information technology department rather than a feature of next generation catalogues. This is discussed in further detail in Chapter 6. What is interesting or noteworthy is that while live chat can be placed within our existing catalogues, it is the excitement and perspective that next generation catalogues bring to a library catalogue that often provide the incentive and vision to add a chat widget to the catalogue.

While these examples demonstrate only the easiest and most basic of reference needs, it is a true representation of the potential that social catalogues have in enhancing reference services and efficiency at the reference desk. As a result, it indicates that reference staff need to consider the role social catalogues can play in their services.

THE LIBRARY COLLECTION

Our library collection is not a core library service, but it is the main beneficiary of social catalogues. The adoption and use of various forms of social software within the public library have increased the accessibility and discoverability of collections that often go unnoticed or are neglected. While DVDs, books, and downloadable collections continue to gain popularity with borrowers, social technology is allowing librarians to creatively explore marketing and promotional opportunities for low-circulating collections. This includes public libraries' music collections. As a result of these new technologies and the features they offer, music collections are gaining more attention and are benefiting from the interactive, social environment that these technologies provide. In an effort to better understand how next generation catalogues are able to promote and market our hidden or often overlooked library collections, this section will focus specifically on music collections to provide concrete examples and explanations.

Social catalogues, or next generation catalogues, offer a variety of ways in which music collections can be discovered in a library's collection. In many public libraries, sound recordings are physically browsed within branches or are found in the catalogue through known item searches. However, they are rarely found in the catalogue through browsing. Social catalogues promote browsing and discovery through faceted navigation. Faceted navigation is the narrowing down of topics by format, subject, or any other category that can be retrieved and sorted through content within the bibliographic record. They also promote browsing through the streaming of cover art. This is often achieved by using prestructured lists created by staff. These prestructured lists are often best-sellers, recommended titles, or "similar" lists. However, it isn't just CDs that can be discovered through these enhanced features.

Printed music, often a format in public libraries that is difficult to access and is often associated with low circulation, can be found by a variety of means by using discovery tools. Many social catalogues not only incorporate faceted navigation but also provide images that visually represent all of the formats associated with a given search term. Rather than merely displaying cover art, if a user searches "Rachmaninoff," the results retrieved may include a display of icons at the top of the page depicting printed music, books, sound recordings, and additional formats representing collections that include items by or about Rachmaninoff. Choosing a format, the facets allow users to narrow down their search by categories such as author, title, date of publication, genres, or subject headings. And, with a "bread crumb" trail, it is easy to track back to the original search. This is especially useful when finding similar items, such as choosing a format and narrowing down first by instrument and then by period. It can also be used as another way to browse for similar titles.

Noteworthy in many of these next generation catalogues is the ability for a search term to call up translations of that term. For music collections, which are often represented in a variety of languages, this provides the user with a powerful tool in recalling items in multiple languages, based on a single search term. In addition to translations, spelling variants or difficult terminology is also an issue with music collections. The "Did you mean . . .?" feature is especially helpful when dealing with difficult spellings or variations of composers' names and music terminology.

Similar to LibraryThing or Del.icio.us, users can tag items, creating custom access points, or search using someone else's tags, which populate the catalogue and therefore enhance access. If your library doesn't have a resident music expert, this also allows local musicians and connoisseurs to add value to existing bibliographic records by applying key access points that cataloguers may not have used. In a public library setting, this is useful because there is not always a music expert or a cataloguer with musical knowledge among the staff. Often, however, it must be noted that tagging can be motivated by personal usage, which leads to tags that do not appear relevant to the larger library community. Understanding the origins of tags and if they are user generated or populated from other sources and the relevancy and ranking that is applied to these tags all play a role in their success or failure.

For cataloguers and reference librarians, the ability to tag has bypassed some of the difficulty that has traditionally occurred with the use of uniform headings. Uniform headings, while extremely beneficial for collection and purposes of organizing information, often aren't the "popular" name of a work. At other times, the uniform title of an item does not represent all of the musical compositions within that one item. This is especially true for sound recordings. Through the use of tagging, as well as facets, users can find all of the recordings, reference resources, or printed music available in the collection associated with a piece or musician and keep those found things found through a variety of options.

One of the most useful uses of tags is the ability to sort them to create additional categories by which to search music collections. They include mood, theme, geographical region, and song titles in addition to the traditional artist name, album, or genre.

With the invitation of user-generated information, reviews can also be written by users and found within the library catalogue. This is especially useful if sound clips to musical recordings are not available for streaming. Reviewers can often relay useful information to other users that may include the quality of the recording or musicians. Others may review scores and discuss the arrangements if parts are missing or if there are issues with the print quality or notation fonts.

Vendors are also offering a variety of enriched content that considers a user's desire to explore items prior to borrowing them. Naxos Music Library (as well as others) allows for live music streaming for hundreds of thousands of tracks. In addition to streaming the music, users can access notes on the works and biographical information. They can also create their own private playlists of music that they like or that they want to focus on. Public libraries can take advantage of this, offering the community access to such a wide variety of musical recordings that they could never physically collect because of the sheer quantity. The danger, of course, of online collections is that the public library is at the mercy of an outside source to provide continual access. Each company that provides an online site is subject to term contracts. As a result, it is possible for a record company to decide that an online service no longer works for it and then remove the material from the site overnight and hence from the library at the same time. As with many of our other online collections, we are opening ourselves up to the same issues that we face with any of our other subscription databases and online journals.

With the ability to stream music, the personalized lists that reside on a catalogue's site can now be taken a step further and streamed through a home computer or mobile device. Imagine featuring the local symphony's season in a series of linkable, streaming music lists. The possibilities, as they continue to become available, are endless. Even if libraries are not yet ready or able to commit the resources to these specialized features, there are alternatives. A simple, homegrown way to explore similar features is by linking to musician's MySpace sites, which allow streaming or adding links to additional, music specific reviews. If cataloguers are unable to take the time to add this content into the bibliographic record, a library blog could certainly feature posts that include this information and, ultimately, receive user feedback as to its popularity.

With the use of social technology, hidden gems in our collection can be found easily as they display side by side with popular items. One of the key features that these new technologies are allowing libraries to do is to gather related musical formats or themes and bring them together through a variety of methods. These social technologies also allow a sharing of information among musicians and music enthusiasts within the community. Whether a public library chooses a discovery tool, music lists, RSS feeds, or live YouTube performances on their website, it is always in an effort to promote the usefulness of the music collection and the vast array of items available for library patrons.

While music collections in public libraries are often difficult to access and are not the highest-circulating items, social software is allowing another level of discovery and exploration that is almost tactile in nature. Shortly, perhaps, there will be not only live streaming offered through libraries but also downloadable sheet music or one-on-one lessons with musicians currently offered through video recordings. Music collections are at a point of transition within public libraries. Sound recordings are expensive or sometimes impossible to replace when damaged, lost, or stolen; printed music is almost nonexistent; and reference materials and resources are given little or no attention. However, the use of social software and the advancements that are being made are allowing librarians to highlight their music collections as well as providing a way for patrons to discover items that have, up until now, been difficult to access.

CONCLUSION

Many of our library services will be positively influenced by next generation catalogues if we position ourselves to take advantage of their features. Throughout this chapter, examples of the variety of ways these catalogues impact specific services have been explored.

While it's easy to look on the implementation of a new catalogue as simply a cosmetic overhaul of our existing legacy catalogues, it soon becomes apparent that next generation catalogues employ powerful features that are waiting to be explored and put to use in a variety of innovative ways. From readers' services to programming, catalogues are a natural companion and partner to assist in carrying out the mandates of our library and core library services.

The examples and scenarios provided within this chapter provide only glimpses into the possibilities of how next generation catalogues can be put to use. One of the more difficult barriers is how to engage staff to accept the strength of the catalogue and to understand the many ways next generation catalogues can be used beyond the traditional definition and standard practices. Encouraging staff to think creatively and to provide them with examples such as the ones provided herein are helpful in exploring how social catalogues and their features can be used to benefit your unique library and the community it serves.

REFERENCES

Smith, Duncan. "Delivering RA Services to Readers in a Digital Age." *Ebooks: Libraries at the Tipping Point* (Library Journal Webcast, September 29, 2010).

Spiteri, L. F. "The Use of Collaborative Tagging in Public Library Catalogues." *Proceedings of the American Society for Information Science and Technology* 43 (2006): 1–5.

CHAPTER 6

Social Features without Social Catalogues: Enhancing Your Public Library Catalogue Is Possible Even with Limitations and Resistance

With all of the excitement and hype surrounding social catalogues in the library world, it is easy to forget that not all libraries are ready, able, or willing to adopt or accept next generation catalogues. While it is easy to be critical of management and professionals who question the purpose of social catalogues, their usefulness, and their impact on the quality of metadata in our catalogues, the answer is not as simple as saying it's the result of ignorance or resistance to change.

There are many reasons libraries are hesitating to acquire and implement social catalogues. While we, as a profession, are known for our cautious exploration of new ideas and technology, the adoption of social catalogues requires jumping into technology that is still highly controversial among librarians and patrons. In addition to its controversial position that often centers around inviting users to generate information that is not completely controlled by libraries, the technology is new. Although its newness is enough to make many professionals hesitate, there are very little research and statistics available to support its functions and usefulness within a library environment. As a result, most professionals are forced into waiting because of funding shortages, hesitations from management, limited resources, and a lack of technological abilities.

While the controversies and concerns over social catalogues from the frontline and backroom perspectives of the profession have been discussed earlier in this book, there is more to adopting a social catalogue than buy-in from staff. Many cataloguing departments and frontline staff are faced with opposing views as to the library "vision" or role in the community.

In many cases, projects for the upcoming years have already been decided on in their strategic plans and funds or resources have been allocated elsewhere.

However, even faced with limited resources, software, funds, or other factors, professionals are still eagerly seeking ways to enhance their services through social features in the catalogue. And they are doing this in innovative ways. Unfortunately, as excited as many of us are to enhance our catalogues, we don't know where to begin or what types of features we can enhance.

This chapter will not only address some of the challenges that prevent professionals from implementing social catalogues but also provide ideas for enhancing the library catalogue without significant costs or resources. While all professionals, both frontline and backroom, can easily practice these ideas or build on them for use in their libraries, this chapter will likely be very helpful for public libraries who want to provide additional benefits and service to their patrons but who lack the resources and budgets for purchasing or implementing their own social catalogue.

LACK OF RESOURCES

One of the biggest factors affecting the acquisition and implementation of next generation catalogues is money. This is not something that can be shied away from or ignored. Whether it is a vendor-based or open-source library catalogue, all of them cost money in the form of budget demands, staff time, and expertise. As a result, whether or not our libraries want a new catalogue, we are often forced to manage with our existing legacy catalogue and our in-house resources.

This is an issue that has been raised in many discussion forums, such as AUTOCAT, as well as in conference sessions, professional literature, and webinars. Where bigger library systems can afford social catalogues, smaller library systems or those without sufficient resources cannot. At this time, it is really only the larger public library systems and wealthy systems that have the leisure to make a decision on acquiring a next generation catalogue, while the remaining libraries have the decision made for them through a lack of financial resources. While this barrier may be somewhat diminished as the newness of the software fades, it will likely remain a major factor for many years to come. We can still see this in the limited choices libraries have when choosing an integrated library system (ILS) vendor. A small market with a handful of players has more control over price than a market with a vast number of competitors. However, open-source software is increasingly providing alternative options in this regard.

Open-source software provides an attractive alternative but it must be recognized that while there is no purchase price for the software, there remains a cost. This cost is tied up in the resources used for cleaning up bibliographic records and implementing the open-source software. With the downsizing of staff in libraries, particularly in the information technology (IT) department, it is difficult to find staff who can install and maintain open-source programs. It is widely acknowledged, even by open-source gurus such as Nicole Engard of ByWater Solutions, that the cost of open-source software is found in its initial application. Libraries that do not have the in-house expertise to implement, customize, and continue to upgrade the software often end up contracting out software assistance. IT specialists with the right expertise do not come cheap. This places another barrier on libraries seeking to acquire social catalogues and discovery tools.

It is not just budget shortages that provide a barrier to acquiring a next generation catalogue or discovery tool. While larger systems often have in-house cataloguing and IT staff, smaller libraries often rely on consortiums for their records and technology support. Rural libraries, many of which would benefit greatly from social catalogues, are often the most limited in staff resources. Implementing vendor-based discovery tools, such as Bowker's AquaBrowser or Innovative Interface's Encore, require significant time and expertise on the library end.

Bibliographic records need to be "cleaned up" and edited for errors in key fields, and at least one IT staff member needs to be available to assist with technical troubleshooting, such as importing and exporting records, firewall issues, access to the database server, and so on. And these are potentially easier products to install because they are available "right out of the box." Additional customization is optional. Smaller libraries do not have the luxury of a large staff. We are all aware that many professionals wear numerous hats, especially in these smaller libraries, with all cataloguing being outsourced. How many of us have played the IT role, which usually consists of basic troubleshooting when it comes to misbehaving printers or computer errors? We can acknowledge that for each specialization in the library comes a specialized set of skills. When we wear numerous hats, not only do we not have the time to spend on implementing new software, but we don't have the necessary expertise.

SYSTEM AND TECHNICAL SHORTCOMINGS

Cataloguers and professionals who support the advent of next generation catalogues often let their excitement overshadow the fact that many libraries, even large ones, outsource their cataloguing. Even if cataloguing is still performed in-house, many find their existing bibliographic records fall short of standard cataloguing practices, accuracy, and detail. Many have older legacy catalogue systems or firewalls and servers that cannot support next generation catalogues.

Without the in-house expertise to edit or clean up old or short bibliographic records, adding a discovery tool or social catalogue will present its own challenges. When Halifax Public Libraries was in the process of implementing AquaBrowser, the records for music scores had to be edited to reflect the correct coding in the leader. The information in the leader, the 000 field in a bibliographic or "MARC" record, determines the format of the item. In this case, rather than indicating that it was printed music, the majority of codes were incorrect, indicating that it was a manuscript. If corrections were not made to this code, the faceted navigation feature, which can visually represent collections and the amount of items in collections, would have incorrectly represented the true number of printed music items in the library's collection. As a result, poor catalogue codes could have indicated that the library had only a handful of musical scores, when in fact their collection had much more. It is this type of work that needs to be completed in order to successfully implement and support a social catalogue. Because the purpose of social catalogues is to allow discovery of a library's entire collection, it also exposes the errors in your bibliographic records. Many library professionals know this and must deal with the inaccuracies in their records before they can implement a social catalogue.

The problem here is twofold. If you have an in-house cataloguing department and you need to clean up the records prior to implementing a discovery tool, critics of the catalogue question why the library has a cataloguing department if the quality of the records is lacking. Why not outsource? However, most of these critics are often unaware of the change in cataloguing practices since the start of automation, including the addition of genre headings and subject headings to fiction collections. The inaccuracies or problem records often reflect older items in the collection that were added shortly after automation.

However, if a library decides to implement a social catalogue without the benefit or ability of cleaning up their bibliographic records, the purpose of the new discovery tool is compromised. Patrons notice a lack of uniformity, format and spelling errors, and access issues. In fact, newer catalogues take our bibliographic records and expose their errors like a microscope examining the follicles on a piece of hair.

Public libraries that have attempted to implement social catalogues without the benefit of clean records or in-house cataloguing expertise often find the process disheartening through the many difficulties that are encountered along the way. Rather than a six- to 10-month implementation process, libraries find themselves invested in a two-year process because of errors involved in initial implementation decisions that provide important criteria outlining what is needed to properly install a discovery tool. This includes facet order, proper leader information for indicating formats, and results display issues, such as weighting and short bibliographic display options.

Although bibliographic records may pose challenges for implementation, they are not insurmountable. However, they have caused many libraries to hesitate when rumours spread of the long and difficult implementation process they may be facing.

Another challenge libraries often face are homegrown ILS systems. Usually developed and maintained within their own IT department, they allow for local customization but may not provide the stability or features necessary for compatibility or sustainability of a social catalogue. This is often because they are built on the backbone of traditional ILSs. While their strong IT departments and internal expertise make them excellent candidates for social catalogues, their systems are not always structured to allow for discovery overlays, such as Encore or AquaBrowser. For example, libraries with homegrown ILSs often have the in-house expertise, and a level of flexibility for customization that many libraries would find envious. However they don't have an authority database, which provides a wealth of uniform and consistent information within discovery tools and during the installation process.

Authority databases are vital in providing a layer of discovery within social catalogues. Until an authority database can be created, implementing any type of front-end social catalogue or discovery tool is not only difficult but perhaps a waste of resources as well. Without the ability to search and sort by authorities, enabling users to search or choose by categories such as series, names, and topics, a social catalogue with its faceted navigation feature would be lacklustre at best.

Libraries who may be interested in adopting a social catalogue may also face challenges with their security settings, such as an inability to bypass their firewall or a lack of server space. The Library of Congress, eager to implement a social tagging experiment for bibliographic and authority records, is currently struggling with their firewall restrictions. At the time this book is being written, they are able to allow tagging only for items placed on a server outside of the firewall. In the case of vendor-related software, vendors must be able to bypass a library's firewall in order to have access to your server for implementation purposes.

I'M *NOT* CONVINCED, SO THE ANSWER IS NO

You've brought in vendors to demonstrate the various social catalogues that you believe are the best options for your library, provided statistics, crunched numbers, and, with a touch of excitement, rattled off projects and goals that could be achieved with a new catalogue. But was it enough?

"I'm not convinced" are three words every professional dreads hearing after pitching one's ideas for implementing a social catalogue. It doesn't matter what follows those three words because it is usually at that moment you realize that, for this year at least, a social catalogue will not make it on the list for the library's strategic plan. These three words usually come out of your director's mouth or another key player on your library board or management team. While many of us focus on the need to convince our cataloguers about the usefulness and benefits of social catalogues, it can be equally if not more difficult to persuade the library decision makers.

While it is important to realize there are many steps you can take to implement social or enhanced features in your catalogue without actually having a social catalogue (and therefore all hope is not lost if your library catalogue does not make the priority list for library projects), the road to a final "no" is a long one. By the time you reach this point, all avenues and opportunities for convincing your library decision makers should be exhausted. For every professional, there are different levels of how far or hard you can push before you decide to accept the final "no," but once you have reached it, a new plan should form in your head. Rather than believing you have hit a dead end, it's time to get creative and rethink how you can use the tools and expertise you already have to enhance your library catalogue. And these enhancements should benefit not only your patrons but staff as well.

IMPLEMENTING SOCIAL FEATURES INTO A LEGACY CATALOGUE

Whatever scenario is being played out at your library, the end result is that, at this time, your library isn't able to acquire and launch a social catalogue. However, rather than believe that this is the end, there are many features and enhancements that can be added to the library catalogue without the benefit of a social catalogue or discovery tool.

Rather than overlaying the library catalogue with an interactive interface or replacing it with a next generation catalogue altogether, local enhancements to the catalogue fall into two categories: enriched bibliographic content and enhanced technological features or abilities.

What projects or ideas have been discussed in your library? Can you think of ways the catalogue can enhance or assist with them? When deciding which features are best for your library catalogue, examining the reasons behind their implementation and the resources that they will require is just as important as if you were purchasing a social catalogue. This is not easy. Does it enhance the user experience or assist staff? Can it help with programming? Will it aid in reference or readers' services? What types of enhancements are available?

There is a wealth of creative ideas for enhancing our library catalogues without undertaking the implementation of a "true" social catalogue. It is worth considering that a library may be better off implementing enhanced features into the catalogue rather than actually acquiring a next generation catalogue or discovery layer. This is a decision that should be based on a library's needs, strategic plan, vision, and resources. Above all, whatever features that are added to enhance the library catalogue should work, be supported fully, and provide meaningful benefits for both patrons and staff.

There are four steps that can help determine what social features and enhancements can be added to the library catalogue.

1. Look at what other libraries are doing but exploring other libraries' catalogues and what vendors are proposing, offering, or working on.
2. Research. Read articles and blogs and follow online forums for ideas and examples of what is being done, how it's being done, and if it can be done. While articles often provide success stories, blogs and forums often provide insight into the difficulties that were encountered, lessons learned, and how they would do things differently if they could begin again.
3. Consider the resources needed to carry out these enhancements. Does your library have the necessary resources to sustain or implement these enhancements?
4. Talk to other professionals.

One of the main purposes of social catalogues is encouraging social interaction, the sharing of information and ideas, and generally contributing to the experience of using the library and its catalogue as an extension of its physical space. The following are some ways to create this experience.

READING LISTS

Many libraries now add live reading lists created by readers' advisors to the library catalogue. These lists are available on the main page of a library catalogue or the library website, and they link directly into the catalogue. This allows readers to explore lists of titles with similar appeals or characteristics and to find out if those titles are available at their library. Cataloguers and readers' advisors work together to create these reading lists. While RAs focus on specific appeals lists, cataloguers who have readers' advisory training can create genre and thematic lists based on their knowledge of the collection and application of genres. This allows the library to provide numerous current and frequently updated lists that cover a wide range of interests and appeals.

Initially, this feature gives the appearance of being staff and resource intensive, requiring a significant amount of time from staff. While the majority of work occurs initially at the front end, once the bulk of the lists have been created and the quantity of lists grows, reading patterns emerge, and these foundational lists can be built on or used for different readers. While some libraries may have the technological skill to create macros that assist in automating the creation of reading lists based on existing lists, other libraries continue to take the "Ask a Librarian" approach and provide hands-on expertise. This may depend largely on the size of a library and its staff.

A primary concern for creating personalized reading lists is the retention of a readers' personal information or reading preferences. It is the responsibility of the library to determine how much or how little information is retained and will usually follow their privacy guidelines. Reading lists do not have to be affiliated with specific readers but can be stored in a database or repository for use with other patrons or as resources to build additional lists for reading recommendations.

Libraries can also invite patrons to submit reading lists, featuring them on the main page of the catalogue or website, with direct links into the catalogue. This is similar to the user-generated lists found in Amazon and creates a feeling ownership and contribution among users of the library.

Linking reading lists into the catalogue is not a difficult task. If a list of titles and a reading list name is provided to a cataloguer, it is a simple matter of identifying a MARC field in a bibliographic record that is not being used and earmarking it as an identifier for reading lists. In Horizon libraries, the 449 tag is often designated as the reading list tag, and therefore the reading list title is added in that field to all the titles belonging on the list. For example, if the library wanted to create a recommended reading list for readers who enjoyed *Suite Française* by Irène Némirovsky, each title on the list would have a 449 MARC tag added to it with the list name inserted. In this case, it would look like this:

449 _ _ $a *If you liked Suite Française . . .*

If the readers' advisory team in the library wanted to create a series of reading lists but Adult Services wanted to create a series of best-selling lists for adults, a cataloguer could create prefixes for each services team list to keep them organized so that duplicate lists are not created. Here is an example:

Readers' Advisory Lists
449 _ _ $a **RA:** Best of Nonfiction 2009
449 _ _ $a **RA:** Best of Nonfiction 2010

Adult Services Lists
449 _ _ $a **AS:** Fiction Bestsellers
449 _ _ $a **AS:** Adult Mysteries

With the help of IT staff, users of the library catalogue can also stumble on these embedded lists if they are made visible in the bibliographic record. If a patron just happens to be looking at the book *The Year is '42* by Nella Bielski, he or she might notice that it belonged to the *If you liked Suite Française* book list. As a live link, a user can then be taken to similar recommended titles for his or her discovery. This is a feature that creates a "no dead end" feel, which allows users to navigate through book lists rather than subjects or genres.

PERSONALIZED ANNOTATED SUMMARIES

Libraries have always talked about trust. Trust has built the foundation for the relationship between libraries and communities. This trust leads readers to share special, personalized reading experiences with us and to have faith in our abilities to suggest reading materials, provide desirable library programming, and to fulfill information needs. Many patrons attend our physical library branches because they have built a relationship with staff. They enjoy entering into discussions with us and value our expertise and opinions. Nowhere is this more apparent than in readers' advisory services, where readers rely on staff to suggest reading recommendations or to express their opinion on books.

Personalized annotated summaries take the trust that patrons place in library staff within the physical branch and put it in the library catalogue. They do this through creating in-house summaries for books and integrating them into bibliographic records.

While it is neither recommended nor practical to create personalized summaries for all of the items in a library's collection, many readers' advisors have been using this feature to promote appeals in their reading lists. Summaries taken from the publisher or book jackets are similar to the subject heading and genre headings used by cataloguers, offering an unemotional, attractive description to appeal to a large audience. It describes what the book is about rather than the reading experience it provides.

An active readers' advisory team can create a short, one- to three-sentence summary that includes reading appeal terminology that describes pace, tone, story line, and the writing style. They can also include information about read-alikes or reading recommendations.

For example, a typical annotated summary from an RA would look something like this:

For readers who enjoyed a Tree Grows in Brooklyn, Lullabies for Little Criminals by Heather O'Neill is another story known for its childlike innocence. As a quick read, it is a coming-of-age tale told from the point of a young girl growing up in a dysfunctional family environment. Heartbreaking yet heart-warming, this story will make you laugh out loud and at other times, make you want to protect all children enduring hardship.

The inclusion of these summaries in bibliographic records assists readers who are not physically at a library branch to make informed reading decisions. Indicating strong language, potential language barriers, or specific values, an annotated summary provides another level of RA services that has not, up until this point, been utilized. How many of us have read the book jacket of a title only to be disappointed when we started reading it? Was it the heavy description and level of detail? Was it the tone that the book evoked? These are appeals that can be addressed in summaries and create another level of personalization and value within our library catalogues.

REVIEWS

Reviews, like annotated summaries, offer another level of personalization in our catalogues. Reviews can be written by staff members or patrons and integrated into the library catalogue. With the expertise of your IT staff, templates similar to the ones used for "Suggestions for Purchase" can be created to invite the writing of book reviews by patrons. Inserted into bibliographic records by default or located under the existing reviews often located on the tool bar within the full bibliographic record display, these links invite user-generated information and a chance for local community members to share reading experiences and opinions on items within the collection.

Whatever choice is made for where the link is located, it is inviting patrons to contribute information to the library. With the sense of pride and responsibility felt by some patrons toward the library and an eagerness to share their opinions with others, book reviews offer another interactive forum for contribution by the community.

Although not as efficient as a social catalogue in its immediate integration into the catalogue, these book reviews, once they are submitted by patrons, can be linked into the catalogue just as other reviews by journals and publishers are. A consideration for adding this feature, however, is the commitment by IT staff to assist with the technical requirements to make this work. Can you batch upload these book reviews? Will it be updated once a week? Or, does each review have to be manually inserted into each record? These are technical decisions and challenges that must be met and addressed by each individual library, often depending largely on in-house expertise, time, commitment to the project, and system capabilities.

ENHANCING INFORMATION IN THE BIBLIOGRAPHIC RECORD (EMBEDDED READING LISTS, CREATION OF NEW GENRE HEADINGS, APPEALS TERMINOLOGY, AND TABLES OF CONTENTS)

Whether personalized annotated summaries, book reviews, or reading lists are integrated into the library catalogue, they all essentially fit into one category: enriching the information found within the bibliographic record.

Each feature that has been discussed up until this point allows a significant amount flexibility to the degree in which each new service is implemented. They are based on building a level of personalization and continuing the trust between staff and patrons found within the physical library branch, promoting a "local" feeling within the catalogue intended to create a comfortable and personal environment for discovery within the library catalogue similar to the feeling experienced in person.

There are examples of libraries throughout North America that have implemented these features successfully. Some have implemented and customized these features to the highest degree, while others have only attempted a feature or two at their most rudimentary level. Even these libraries that have only begun implementing very simple and basic enhanced features into their catalogue are providing benefits to their users. Any addition, whether it is a simple personalized summary or a reading list with recommendations, will enhance a users' experience with the library catalogue.

There are also libraries, such as Hennepin County Library, that have taken their legacy catalogue and website and integrated them to a point where the services they offer are seamless, interactive, and almost unrecognizable from the out-of-the-box, standard legacy catalogues that most libraries are still using. However, other libraries, such as Halifax Public Libraries and Edmonton Public Library, continue to offer these enhanced services on a more moderate basis using resources comparable to most average-sized public library systems. In addition to reading lists, summaries, and reviews, there are other, more basic enhancements that can be integrated into cataloguing practices that will be reflected in bibliographic records.

It was only a handful of years ago that works of fiction, if catalogued at all, included nothing more than genre headings as access points. In fact, there are still libraries today that do not assign subject headings to their fiction titles, preferring to add the more generic genre headings and thereby relying on those headings, in combination with known item searches of authors or titles, to locate reading ideas for users of the library. In libraries with an active readers' advisory team, that practice is considered antiquated and not at all useful for leisure readers. With minimal effort and without a significant increase in the time it takes to catalogue a work of fiction, cataloguers began inserting subject headings and summaries into these bibliographic records, enhancing access, increasing findability, and assisting readers in finding items that are relevant to them, beyond a known item search or broad genre.

Works of fiction are not the only items benefitting from increased data in bibliographic records. While nonfiction titles traditionally include subject headings, they lack some very relevant and useful information, namely, the table of contents. Today, cataloguers actively insert the table of contents information into nonfiction works. We take for granted that the majority of nonfiction items include this information, and, if missing, staff and patrons often ask for its addition to our records. While Amazon's "search inside" function is preferable and reflect what patrons have come to expect, adding any additional content that assists patrons in determining if an item is of interest to them remains beneficial.

Cataloguers are increasingly aware of the content that can be provided by other sources and the need for using their expertise for increasing the usefulness of bibliographic records in a variety of ways. This is especially true when facing outsourcing, copy cataloguing, and inserting vendor-supplied information directly into the catalogue. Next generation catalogues provide cataloguers more opportunities for enhancing the catalogue in a multitude of additional ways that have previously been neglected or unrecognized.

In the area of readers' services, new genres and buzzwords constantly arise and evolve. By collaborating, cataloguers can incorporate many of these headings into the library catalogue. This is especially important if readers and readers' advisors are using these new buzzwords to search for reading ideas in the catalogue. Working collaboratively with the readers' advisory team, new, localized genre headings that are not currently reflected in catalogues and not "authorized" Library of Congress or Library and Archives Canada authorities can be created and adopted as localized genre headings that benefit access to a library's collection. An example of this can be found in the increasing popularity of narrative nonfiction works. While narrative nonfiction is a difficult concept to define and apply to books, the genres that fall under it, such as memoirs, microhistories, true crime, and reporting, are not. Working on team projects and including cataloguers on those teams allow frontline staff to take advantage of what the catalogue has to offer and opportunities to open a dialogue for continuous improvement. With the frontline staff actively interacting with users and witnessing firsthand reading preferences and trends, they can take advantage of a cataloguer's expertise in enhancing the catalogue for improving access by sharing these words and the terminology. Not only does this take away the all-too-familiar frustration staff feel when searching the catalogue with a current term and retrieving no results, it also reflects local and community needs, reading patterns, and terminology. Looking at this from a broader perspective, this type of collaboration and the results that can occur resemble the usefulness of social tagging in social catalogues. Many times, the folksonomies created by users assist cataloguers in determining new or useful subject headings that are adopted as "authorized" formal headings for bibliographic records. If a library catalogue cannot offer tagging for its users, staff can play a role in making cataloguers aware of these terms.

Another recently considered enhancement to the library catalogue is the addition of appeals terminology to bibliographic records. Appeals terminology are words often used to describe the tone, story line, writing style, and pace of titles. Although appeals terms can often be added to a local summary, those words are not part of a standardized vocabulary, making searching for them difficult. However, if a standardized, controlled vocabulary is created and added as an access point, readers and readers' advisors would have an abundance of searchable items to help readers find books of interest to them and assist staff in making reading recommendations and creating book lists.

Finally, there is one more feature worth mentioning briefly when it comes to enhancing the library catalogue: linking. This includes linking to our website, linking to author readings, linking to our readers' services blog, or linking to online PDFs or alternate versions of our titles. This goes back to one of the founding ideas for next generation catalogues: *no dead ends*. No dead ends is about allowing patrons to discover and explore without being led to a bibliographic record that doesn't allow further exploration. Live links to reviews are already part of our catalogues. Including reading lists that are live links has already been discussed and is another way to provide this. But providing links in and out of the catalogue or throughout the catalogue and the library website are integral in pulling all relevant information together. A popular book that has local author reading, especially if it is part of a featured reading list, benefits from a link located in the bibliographic record directing a reader to the information about the author reading. If the library's readers' services team maintains a blog and is highlighting a book list, links to the blog (and a link from the blog to the catalogue) can also be added.

While, admittedly, most of the enhancements that have been discussed up until this point are in the area of readers' services, it is because it is a service that is continually gaining popularity within libraries. These enhancements are also simple to adopt and insert into bibliographic records. With the rise of Google and other sources of information, libraries have been promoting and growing the one service that cannot, at this time, be offered anywhere else: assisting patrons with finding the right movie, music, or book to fit their preferences and mood.

While it is easy to promote social catalogues and all that they add to the library catalogue experience, the word "social" is a misnomer. Next generation catalogues are about providing patrons with what they want. It is not just about providing them with a means of sharing reading experiences, creating lists, or interacting with others. While user-generated information plays a large role, next generation catalogues aren't about a specific piece of software; rather, they're about how we look at library catalogues and what we decide to put into them. Adding subject headings for works of fiction, creating local headings, and adding tables of contents to nonfiction titles are examples of how we see the catalogue as a useful tool rather than an inventory. With this in mind, the possibilities of how to improve and re-create the library catalogue as a place for discovery and experience are endless.

ADDING ENHANCEMENTS WITH TECHNOLOGY

It is easy to focus all of the attention on the library catalogue and how much information we can provide in its bibliographic records. There are some considerations that need to be addressed, however. While many traditional patrons may enjoy searching the catalogue, it is not the only media our patrons are using to access our collections. In fact, many younger patrons have no desire to visit the library catalogue except to place a hold on an item or go directly to a topic that interests them. "Be where your patrons are" is a slogan that is often repeated in the library world when pitching marketing ideas for attracting more patrons. We know where many of our patrons are because we're there too. We have Blackberries, iPhones, and hold accounts on Facebook. Many of us have personalized iGoogle pages or subscribe to RSS feeds. Does your library catalogue have a presence there?

Many libraries have created teen pages on Facebook. Readers' advisors have created blogs for reading ideas. Has anyone thought to link the library catalogue to these resources or to link these sources to the library catalogue, with the library catalogue being the main source of entry into the library?

Public libraries have started using widgets to create a library catalogue search box that users can place on their iGoogle home pages. With a staff member who has basic HTML knowledge, the library can create another window into the library catalogue on the most popular search engine in the world. Local users can just add this widget as they do the news or weather and place it on their home page. Every time they are on their home page, the library catalogue search box is there for their convenience. Is it worth the user to then search first for the Amazon Web page and then the site for the book they are thinking about? Or will those users decide to conveniently search the book from their home page, leading them right into the local library catalogue?

MOBILE DEVICES AND RSS FEEDS

With the increasing reliance on our mobile devices, it is only natural to seek ways to improve access to our catalogues through the use of cell phones. To address this, public libraries are creating a simplified version of their library catalogues that are more friendly in their display than the default catalogue page. Libraries are also finding new and inventive ways to add RSS feeds for patrons to subscribe to both on their home pages and via their mobile devices.

Books from favourite genres, newly added materials, or alerts that the patrons hold are now available for pickup and are new and inventive ways libraries are interacting with patrons. All without the benefit of a social catalogue, libraries are finding ways to interact with users and provide them with the information they want wherever they are. RSS feeds and news alerts, such as the ones often used by Twitter, blogs, email providers, and Facebook, provide libraries with a variety of ways to connect with users and provide them with the "boiled-down," specific information they are looking for.

EMBEDDED REFERENCE AND RA CHAT IN THE CATALOGUE

Recently, libraries have been taking advantage of Web 2.0 technology by getting creative with live chat. Libraries have been adding live reference chat, (often called "Ask Us" or "Ask a Librarian,") using free chat widgets such as Meebo, into the catalogue. And why not? Traditionally, reference chat has been available only through the library website. But where do our patrons need the most assistance? Often, it is when they are searching in the library catalogue. Rather than choosing an either/or situation where the chat widget is located in one place only, libraries can use these free, open-source software products to enhance the catalogue and provide chat opportunities in a variety of places.

Similar to the logo or branding that appears throughout the catalogue, chat widgets can be added as a stationary feature, found even in the full bibliographic record displays. When patrons are searching in the catalogue and have questions or can't find what they are looking for, the chat widget is easily available from wherever they are in the library catalogue. This enhancement simplifies the chat process, requiring patrons not to return to the website but to immediately have the opportunity to chat with or send a question to library staff.

Although not currently practiced in libraries, another option is to split reference chat with readers' services chat. A reader can be in his or her home or sitting at the airport and still receive assistance in finding a book to read. As a result, readers' advisors can conduct an RA interview remotely, which is not currently done. In many libraries, readers' advisors outnumber reference staff. With the additional staffing available, sustaining such a service allows RAs throughout the library system to participate. Ultimately this not only takes advantage of sharing resources but also provides a unique, practical, and beneficial service to the library community.

ENRICHED CONTENT THROUGH VENDORS

Syndetics Solutions

There is a significant amount of in-house enhancements that can be added to library catalogues to make them feel more "social" rather than static and unfriendly. However, they require a level of time, commitment, and expertise that library management may not be willing to expend, even if they are in favour of the general idea. For libraries that aren't quite ready to commit themselves to social catalogues but still have the resources to commit funds to software or catalogue enhancements, vendors do provide some very exciting features that can be implemented in both legacy and next generation catalogues.

Syndetic Solutions is likely the most well known vendor among libraries for offering enriched content packages. Compatible with virtually every ILS, Syndetics Solutions offers public libraries the opportunity to enhance their catalogues, even if the actual cataloguing is not performed in-house. Because it is an "add-on" feature, it acts as another layer to your catalogue rather than embedding the data directly into the MARC record. The content is integrated with a library's ILS by matching the ISBN and is then displayed in the catalogue by use of XML coding or through HTML pop-up windows.

Syndetics Solutions content is no stranger to public libraries, with most already subscribing to packages that provide cover art, summaries, reviews, and tables of contents. However, many patrons accustomed to online book-stores find this as a common feature. Instead, they have higher expectations of the library catalogue than the ability to search inside the book, read the first chapter, or find read-alikes for popular or favourite books. These options and many others are offered in Syndetics' enriched content packages.

Even with all of the positive enhancements offered by Syndetics Solutions, it is not without its shortcomings. As an American-based company, content from other countries, such as Canada, is not often reflected in their enriched content packages. It is important that public libraries outside of the United States understand this, especially if they are seeking a way to promote local material or material published within their own country. Some cataloguing departments, to circumvent this shortcoming, are adding the ISBN that originates out of the United States. For example, most DVDs released in Canada have a unique ISBN issued out of their place of manufacture or distribution. This is usually Canada. The cover art to these DVDs, despite being popular, box-office movies, do not display in the public library catalogue. However, by adding the American issued ISBN to the MARC record, the image of that DVD will display.

While all of this enriched content is valuable if a user is looking at a specific record, up until recently, none of Syndetic Solutions's enriched content was searchable in the library catalogue. However, in June 2007, they launched their newest product, Syndetics Ice, in order to address this issue. Syndetics Ice allows the enriched content, such as tables of contents, summaries, and reviews, to be searched.

In addition to providing the ability to search the common enriched content, they have taken their product and explored the readers' advisory aspect. Throughout this book, there has been an emphasis on the relationship that must be encouraged and developed between readers' services and cataloguing. Many of the in-house enhancements that have been discussed in this chapter deal with this collaborative relationship and the benefit to users. Syndetic Solutions, in their new product, has also explored the relationship with readers' services and the catalogue with its ability to provide read-alike suggestions for titles based on the library's collection. If a title is currently unavailable or there is a large holds list, users have the ability to link into a customized Fiction Connection that is based on the collection at the subscribing library.

With the many features and options available through Syndetics Solutions, they are a good alternative option for adding enhanced discovery and exploration within the library catalogue. While many libraries have the resources to depend primarily on vendor services, other libraries are finding that a balance between the two suits their needs and their patrons' needs very well.

NoveList Select

One of the founding premises of this book is that the library catalogues currently being developed and those of the future will be much more interactive, dynamic, and social. As those theories are developed into technical realities, library catalogues will have a major impact on workflows and will affect core library services. One of the most popular and fastest-growing services within the library is readers' advisory services. NoveList, a leader in RA services is already addressing this by creating an RA read-alike tool that can be embedded directly into a library's catalogue. Compatible in both legacy catalogues and discovery tools, it displays read-alikes in the bibliographic record. These lists are predetermined by NoveList contributors and not by local staff. As a result, choosing an option such as NoveList Select provides more free time on the staff side, allowing them to focus on other services, projects, or enhancements.

NoveList Select was developed to bring readers' services directly into the library catalogue and therefore directly into readers' homes and schools. The NoveList database is used primarily by professionals at present. Embedding read-alikes within the catalogue will open this resource to patrons as well. As a benefit to staff, rather than having to toggle between the NoveList database and the library catalogue, this provides a "one stop shop" where all of the information is gathered and all of the titles suggested are in the collection. The preexisting NoveList lists are matched with the library's collection, and only those titles in the collection will display. And, more important, rather than taking the patron out of the catalogue into NoveList or some other freestanding software, it displays within the catalogue and lets you link to the suggested title within the catalogue or place a hold.

While creating in-house reading lists and embedding them within the catalogue is an alternative to NoveList Select, the resources demanded on staff time are a consideration. Will staff create in-house reading lists even if NoveList Select is offered in the catalogue? To many, the answer is yes, but the idea that reading recommendations belong in the catalogue and not in external sources is what is notable. To determine how a library will go about doing this is based primarily on individual libraries' needs, resources, and vision.

Library Thing for Libraries

Library Thing for Libraries (LTFL) as well as Amazon provide enriched content to public libraries. LTFL populates a public library catalogue with tags from their online social catalogue, LibraryThing. The reason for this? LibraryThing tags add another layer to the existing access points in bibliographic records. These tags reflect slang, different viewpoints and perspectives, buzzwords, and new terminology that aren't reflected in the standard controlled vocabulary used by cataloguers. LTFL tags also "fill out" bibliographic records that have little or no description, providing enhanced access to items that would otherwise be difficult to discover.

Palmerston North City Library in New Zealand is an example of a public library using LTFL. Displayed in a tag cloud, the terms are represented in a variety of sizes, the boldest terms being the most relevant and the smaller words being less so, as determined by LibraryThing users. The tags within the tag cloud are live, so if a user clicks on a word, a window pops up, providing a list of other items within the collection that include the same tags. While not the same as a read-alike list, it does provide the choice for users to explore similar topical items within the library collection.

There are, however, critics of LTFL. Many are concerned that the tags are irrelevant, inappropriate, uncontrolled, and not representative of the local community. LibraryThing is a global library, with users from around the world. The terminology that has been created is an aggregate of cultures and communities, with the most highly rated and representative being ranked at the top. The majority of inappropriate terms are all but stripped out of the data because of their lack of use and are hardly, if ever, found in public libraries that use LTFL.

FEDERATED SEARCHING

The last enhanced feature that will briefly be mentioned in this chapter is federated searching. At this time, Serials Solutions is the primary vender offering this stand-alone feature. Federated searching allows for a single, unified search for exploring all of a library's holding.

Federated searches are a popular feature of social catalogues and are heavily marketed to libraries that acquire these catalogues because it allows users to search in one place rather than toggling between pages to find all of the libraries' holdings and relevant resources. However, libraries do not have to implement a social catalogue to acquire federated searching. Many libraries purchase federated searching tools for their legacy catalogues, as it not only exposes the many subscription databases within the collection that are often neglected but also is a very public and noticeable enhancement to collection access.

CONCLUSION

It is not necessary for libraries to rely on social catalogues to make their library catalogues into attractive discovery tools. While the "social" side of legacy catalogues will always struggle without the benefit of a customizable discovery tool, there are many options available to professionals who are willing to get creative with the resources available to them. The variety of ideas explored in this chapter should be considered not as a complete list but as a starting point to explore the possibilities available to public libraries for enhancing their catalogues. Enhancing the library catalogue is about creating and providing tools to meet the needs of the community and the staff. It is not about how "shiny" or cutting edge it appears. Online library catalogues provide access to information. While traditionally that has only meant access to a library's holdings, today's catalogues are providing information about those holdings, information from the community, and opinions from a variety of resources. It is now a place to share and generate information as well as access the collection to fulfill individual needs in a capacity that is relevant and useful to a user. The tools that we decide to place within our catalogue should promote that purpose.

CHAPTER 7

Future Directions
of the Library Catalogue

While next generation catalogues have been gaining real popularity in public libraries only within the past five years, it's important to understand that they are not a static technology. Our legacy catalogues have seen only minor adjustments and enhancements to correct minor technology challenges. However, next generation catalogues continue to evolve and develop. This implies that the technology is not only viewed as progressive rather than static but also continually developed and enhanced in order to meet the users' demands and needs. One reason they can do this is because of the relatively easy nature of the catalogues' upgrading process or customization tools for many of these catalogues. As discussed in Chapter 2, rather than a single component among many, the majority of social catalogues used in public libraries are overlays that we apply to our existing OPACs which allow for quick customization and upgrading.

Even with all of the benefits that social catalogues are poised to contribute to library services and users, it has to be acknowledged that much more research and development needs to take place. While this text has focussed primarily on the positive aspects of social catalogues, there are movements among professionals to see even greater improvements made to this technology. Next generation catalogues, as described in the introduction, is a generic term for library catalogues that have moved beyond the technology of our existing legacy catalogues and are meant to serve a greater function within the library. However, next generation catalogues describe not one iteration or generation of a catalogue but rather a new type of catalogue that incorporates features and possibilities that were not possible in the past. As a result, this chapter will focus on some of the areas that still need to be explored with respect to social catalogue technology as well as acknowledging the limited amount of research that we are currently modeling our new catalogues on.

Imagine sitting in a library conference on a session for research on cataloguing issues. It's an hour-and-a-half session examining areas of research that need to be undertaken within the profession to explore the growing and expanding roles of our skills, metadata, cataloguing practices, and library catalogues. It's a packed room, with eager attendees filling the chairs, sitting on the floor, and leaning against the walls busily taking notes. About an hour into the session, the last presenter approaches the podium to present on research needed for examining next generation catalogues. *A good quarter of the room, maybe more, gets up and leaves.*

While we'd like to think this would never happen, I experienced this event at a recent library conference. Even as this book is being written, library and information professionals are talking about a *next* next generation of catalogues, while others in the profession are barely aware of what a first next generation catalogue is. And yet others are dismissing them as a wannabe "Google" phase that will blow over or just another modernization of the catalogue similar to when card catalogues became automated. While these catalogues have been growing in popularity since 2006, many libraries have yet to implement them or, they don't even know they exist.

So why did so many cataloguers, librarians, and managers get up and leave the room when the last speaker was ready to present on research needs for next generation catalogues? While we can jokingly say they were worried the speaker would be boring, they needed to grab a coffee, or they all had another session to attend, there may be a more obvious and yet troubling explanation: it hasn't yet occurred to them that research for next generation catalogues should fall to the practicing professional (nonacademic) or to anyone outside of the information technology (IT) department. While cataloguers are able to understand the direct benefits and implications of research into metadata, data connectivity, data and resource sharing, and cataloguing standards, the structure, features, and uses of next generation catalogues are harder to associate with everyday tasks and needs. Many professionals in the "back room" think of catalogues as a technology issue and not a cataloguing issue. Frontline staff view the catalogue as an IT or cataloguing issue. While the IT department should play a role in the support of catalogues, cataloguers and frontline staff are the professionals directly impacted by what a library catalogue offers.

It is also difficult for many public librarians, including cataloguing librarians, to find the time to involve themselves in research projects or to find opportunities in which they can participate. Traditionally, research is left to the academics, and public libraries simply make do with statistics and voluntary surveys. However, if we want to influence the functions of next generation catalogues, management needs to encourage their librarians to involve themselves in research and allow them to participate in research studies as part of their daily tasks. Many public librarians on discussion forums have provided extremely valuable insight into the shortcomings of next generation catalogues: the appearance of compromises between function and "flash." Developers and vendors have heard us express our wish for catalogues to be more like Google and Amazon, but they haven't heard enough about what our catalogues do extremely well or, at least, what we as professionals believe our catalogues do better than commercial sites. As a result, many of these next generation catalogues have compromised certain long-standing legacy catalogue functions, such as browsing by author or subject, in favour of faceted navigation or more "white space" on our catalogue home page. This is not necessarily the fault of the vendor or the practicing professional but rather the result of a lack of research into social catalogues or library catalogues in general. Although critical, it may also be the result of librarians and managers not necessarily knowing what they want in the library catalogue. While it is easy to say our current catalogues aren't working and so we express our vision for a more "Google-like" catalogue, we aren't acknowledging our own unique position. We aren't Google, we aren't Amazon, and we're definitely not Facebook. Each of these platforms has found a way to use technology and social media to their own advantage in their own unique way and, as a result, enhance their own value and market. Right now, libraries are just reusing this technology, not yet having found our own "voice" or unique way of using this technology in a library environment. We can't expect vendors to know what we need and how these features should be used alongside our existing services if we don't know how or haven't even considered these factors ourselves.

RESEARCH

Whether this book is your first introduction to next generation catalogues or you are already familiar with them, it's important to note that, as with any service we provide or technology we adopt for everyday use in libraries, it needs to be examined. Evidence-based research is significantly lacking in the area of next generation catalogues despite the fact that we are quickly adopting these catalogues for use in our libraries. While it should be recognized that in most cases implementation of these catalogues is an improvement over our legacy or classic catalogues, that does not dismiss the need to conduct proper research into the features of these catalogues and their future role within the library.

At the 2010 American Library Association Conference held in Washington, D.C., Amy Eklund, catalogue librarian at Georgia Perimeter College, presented on the need for additional research focussing on next generation library catalogues. In her presentation, she identified the following four reasons that research is needed:

- A build-it-and-they-will-come approach has been used in its design and implementation.
- Outside discovery tools are not integrated with the catalogue but rather overlay them as an interface.
- Next generation catalogue features are not based on large-scale evidence.
- Rich content contained within library records is not being exploited (Eklund 2010, slide 5).

The research that has recently begun on examining these catalogues and not just social media elements but specifically focussed on these new library catalogues is in its most preliminary stages. Although some vendors acknowledge that they have conducted research and examined the usefulness and need for their product, this information is not made available to the professionals who need it most: the decision makers in libraries who are deciding whether to purchase and implement these catalogues and which is best for them. In fact, without the understanding of how or why we need certain elements within these new catalogues, professionals are either basing their decisions on instinct and research that has been completed in the commercial environment or focussing on social media platforms such as LibraryThing and Del.icio.us.

However, with the increasing amount of libraries implementing these catalogues and implementing social features, I predict that we'll notice an increase in research examining next generation catalogues in the areas that Eklund outlines. Comprehensive usability studies to evaluate the usability of these catalogues among library patrons and staff are essential. In 2011, Louise Spiteri and I concluded a one-year Online Computer Library Center (OCLC)–funded research project examining the use of social catalogues in two major libraries in Canada. My interest and participation in this research stems from an effort to gather evidence that will assist public libraries in making informed decisions about next generation catalogues, what elements are essential, what elements are lacking, and, perhaps, future elements that need to be developed. The first year of research, however, provides the groundwork to these questions. As a result, this specific study focussed on daily transaction logs of the social discovery systems used by two Canadian public libraries. These logs were compiled from May to August 2010. A transaction log is an electronic record of interactions occurring between a system and users. This allows researchers to observe and analyze user behaviours (Jansen, Spink, and Taksa 2009). Edmonton Public Library (EPL) and Halifax Public Libraries (HPL) were chosen as participants in this research. EPL uses the BiblioCommons catalogue, while HPL uses AquaBrowser. While many factors may have contributed to our conclusions in this project, including the fact that EPL's catalogue had been launched less than two years and HPL was still in the process of providing a full marketing campaign to the public, our general conclusion is that both libraries appear to be making limited use of the social features, and as a result client interaction is minimal at best. But what does this say about the success of our catalogues? Can it be that we are not using social features correctly? For example, what motivates a user to interact with our catalogue? Are they going to tag, rate, and review just because we offer it? Will they return to the catalogue to offer a review *after* having read a book, or would they be more likely to contribute if they were an extension of our in-house library services? For example, would users be more motivated to contribute if they belonged to a book club that encouraged this or through online interaction with our readers' advisors? While these topics have been discussed in this book, these are questions that still need to be asked and answers that need to be found.

In the end, research that evaluates the usability of social catalogues will assist vendors in making informed decisions about product development and allow libraries to become informed on what they need and what type of catalogue or features are best for their library. As a result, research and examination into next generation catalogues will provide a record of benchmarks for future growth, informed product development, and informed decision making for libraries.

SOCIAL CONTENT IN LIBRARY CATALOGUES

At this time, and without a sufficient amount of comprehensive evidence regarding the usability of social catalogues, we are basing their development and success on the social media model, which concludes that if users want to tag, rate, review, and share on sites such as LibraryThing, Facebook, and Del.icio.us, they also want to do so in our catalogues. However, what we fail to consider are the reasons behind why users participate in social technologies and communities. Why do users want to participate in social activities online? What motivates them and/or attracts them to choose one technology over another?

While it can be concluded that social technologies will play a significant role in the future success of the library catalogue, what remains to be seen is how these technologies will be used. Will patrons tag in the catalogue like they do in Amazon? Will they want to write reviews? It is entirely possible that while the features of next generation catalogues reflect popular social media technologies, how users and staff make use of them may be completely unique from the models we are basing our assumptions on.

Much of what has been discussed in this book does provide a glimpse into how social technologies can be used in libraries. Rather than following the model of the social media sites, the growing trend may reflect how library staff and users integrate these collaborative features into core library services to enhance our existing practices and the services that patrons expect. It is my hope that this book has introduced a new way of thinking about the use of collaborative tools within a social site. While social media sites rely on users to tag, rate, and review primarily for personal reasons or as a result of a strong opinion (usually motivated by an extremely positive or negative experience concerning the purchase of an item), libraries may find themselves using the features of social catalogues to encourage interaction between book clubs, promoting the next "good read," or assisting with the ESL (English as a second language) community members through collaborative resource list creation.

There are a number of possibilities available for user generated information that needs to be explored by libraries. How do patrons and staff want to use our social functions? Will we find this direction moving away toward the common social media motivations and more toward the practical functions of a library that users expect? In the future, more libraries are likely to explore alternate options for using social features as they find many patrons may not be as keen on using these features as we have expected. Rather than removing these catalogues or doing away with the social aspects of next generation catalogues, we are likely to see an increasing amount of creative thinking and usage of these features that incorporates and focusses on collaboration and community involvement.

MOBILE TECHNOLOGIES

A popular and interesting idea that has been emerging in professional literature is that the library website and catalogue aren't user "destination spots." Rather, our websites and catalogues are found through gateways, being pointed out to an individual by a friend, colleague, application, or some type of outside source. This is different from the concept of what we are used to. Rather than a "build-it-and-they-will-come" approach, we now have to rely on users finding us through social media and links generated by users. Online user traffic is directing patrons to the library through these gateways.

While there will be, for the foreseeable future, individuals who have bookmarked our catalogue on their browsers, an increasing number of users will find us through RSS feeds, smartphone applications, friend recommendations, or a social networking presence (such as Facebook and Twitter). Of interest is how we are addressing this new form of access to our catalogue in an environment of immediacy, brevity, and short attention spans. There is a recent study that explores this idea of convenience as a major factor in information-seeking behaviour (Connaway et al. 2011). In particular, it focuses on convenience as a "situational criterion in peoples' choices and actions during all stages of the information-seeking process. The concept of convenience can include their choice of an information source, their satisfaction with the source and its ease of use, and their time horizon in information seeking" (Connaway et al. 2011).

Within the past year, there has been a marked increase in the availability of mobile applications for library catalogues as vendors and software developers race to develop mobile platforms that users will download or use on their smartphones. This is in direct correlation with the ever-increasing about of smartphone users in North America. And one of the challenging yet fascinating aspects of this growing platform is the difference in how users want their information on a mobile application versus a desktop computer. Users with both smartphones and desktop computers tend to use each technology differently, with the intention that quick searches or brief interactions with technology for the sake of convenience are the purpose of smartphones, while in-depth work, searches, or blogging (content creation) are saved for the desktop computer. This poses a challenge for developers of mobile technologies for library cataloguers.

Screenshot of a library catalogue mobile application on iPhone. Created by HybridForge and implemented at Dallas Public Library.

If a user on a smartphone averages only about 45 seconds on any given mobile application, what are the key elements that a user needs to derive the best experiences and the most use out of the application for the library catalogue? What do users want when they visit our library catalogues on their phone? Heavy text? Big buttons? Limited options with the most popular features highlighted? Likely, one thing they don't want is technology that gets in the way of function. If the loading time for the application is slow—if there are too many words, needless scrolling, or enlarging—then your chances for a successful mobile application are low. We always want to consider the principle of convenience and the motivation behind why users have chosen to use their mobile application over a computer.

Currently, the majority of big-name vendors of our library catalogues are creating a text version of their catalogues, as are the vendors who provide discovery overlays. In essence, they are reverting back to catalogues that are text based and bare boned, which is similar to the interfaces we've been providing to users who have dial-up Internet in rural locations. Rather than learning from what social media have to offer and the reason behind why users are turning to their smartphones, vendors are turning toward what they know and what's worked in the past to provide a mobile platform in an attempt to stay competitive with outside software developers. However, these text-based mobile platforms reflect our legacy catalogues, with small text, drop-down menus, and too many advanced options for the purposes of mobile use.

On the other hand, software developers who are in the mobile application market are taking a look at our catalogues and creating simple, clear, and big-button mobile applications that highlight the most popular features used in our catalogues: reading lists, best-sellers, read-alikes, and placing holds. Some of these applications include ISBN scanning for those patrons in bookstores checking to see if the library already has the item and additional keys for searching title, author, and subject.

What's important to note about the software developers' products is that they take into consideration social media and the user's purpose for choosing to search the catalogue on the smartphone rather than the desktop, while many library vendors are considering only the smaller screen of a phone.

While at this time it appears that outside software developers are far more successful at creating mobile applications than library vendors, this is not necessarily indicative of the future of mobile applications and where libraries will be turning to acquire them. The explosion of mobile platforms and their adoption in libraries has really taken off only in the past year, and the technology is, just like social catalogues, still in its infancy. However, if we can gaze into a crystal ball, it is easy to predict an increasing amount of attention on the development and integration of mobile applications with our library catalogues—both from vendors within the library environment and externally. The future development of these applications

Screenshot of search results page on a mobile application for iPhone. Note the simple, clear and intuitive interface. Created by HybridForge and implemented at Dallas Public Library.

will incorporate key features from our social catalogues. What I envision are mobile applications that are able to extract data from several library sources to seamlessly offer users what they want. This may mean pulling data from the library's blog as well as highlighting the latest patron reviews so that a user who views the best-seller list on his or her smartphone will also see the latest blog post on the item, perhaps even presenting related library events, the latest user reviews, and content from a readers' advisory source, such as NoveList or even LibraryThing, that also provides a list of similar titles. And all of this will be displayed with a presentation that reflects that the interface was designed for a smartphone rather than modified from an online interface.

Screenshot of details page on mobile application for iPhone. Created by HybridForge and implemented at Dallas Public Library.

Even with the newness of smartphones, there have been early adopters of this technology for libraries. Examples of these libraries include the Edmonton Public Library which launched a mobile application for their catalogue created by BiblioCommons in the late summer of 2010, and the Ouachita Parish Public Library, which acquired a mobile application that was created for their library from Hybrid Forge, a Web development and e-commerce consulting company that has taken an interest in creating mobile platforms for libraries.

While one library decided to implement a library vendor's mobile application (BiblioCommons) and the other chose an outside software development company (Hybrid Force), both libraries acknowledged the need for the platform to be created for smartphones rather than an adaptation of an existing online interface.

However, even with many libraries exploring the possibility of mobile interfaces, many professionals hesitate to commit resources into acquiring these mobile applications until they can provide service to all smartphones, including Blackberry, Android, and Apple products. Like the naysayers of the social catalogue, librarians and management point to a lack of tech-savvy users or a need to focus on the disenfranchised or existing user base. The response we can give is also similar to that given in a previous chapter. The growth rate and the adoption of smartphone usages is increasing quarterly. This technology is becoming the most highly adopted technology in history and represents a large portion of our taxpayers and future taxpayers who aren't necessarily using our libraries, that is, the majority of working professionals, and the Generation X and Y populations.

The ability to create one mobile application across smartphone platforms will increase and develop over time. But to not serve any smartphone customers or to provide mobile sites that reflect our legacy catalogues while we wait to acquire true mobile applications may be more of an issue. Is it better to provide what appears to be outdated interfaces for display on new technology tools? Or is it better to adopt new technology, knowing that at this time you are serving only a portion of your customers but will eventually support all of your customers? It rather mimics many libraries' decisions to acquire Overdrive even while they could be used on only half of the devices available to users. Over time, the number of devices that are supported has increased, as will the platforms that mobile applications will be available for.

Mobile applications for next generation catalogues will continue to grow in the forthcoming years. Research into these catalogues will provide meaningful data into what features are essential in library catalogues and provide guidance into which of those features should be reflected in their mobile counterparts. In the meantime, software developers both within and outside the library will take advantage of the growth in popularity of smartphones and continue to explore how, why, and when users will use the applications and when they will choose to sit down at their desktops to visit our library catalogues.

MARKETING

With the concept of accessing the library and its online services through gateways, it follows that our marketing strategies need to address the new ways we need to reach our users and nonusers. Many of our existing patrons will continue to visit our library websites and catalogues no matter what we do. They already use our services, they continue to use our services, and, most likely, they will use our services into the future. While we can offer them enhanced services, social media are key components in marketing our next generation catalogues. The mistake many libraries often make is using traditional marketing methods. Radio and television advertisements, bookmarks, and T-shirts all serve a purpose but aren't addressing the new destination spots of users. They certainly aren't attracting new, tech-savvy users. Many libraries are aware of this, often using their Twitter feeds and Facebook pages to promote new services as well. But again, is this the best way to attract new users or to promote a next generation catalogue that purports to be wherever the users are? When we think about gateways, we have to think about where users are entering our library from or who and what is directing them to us. Taking advantage of venues and platforms that provide visibility and possible uses of a next generation catalogue to users will likely play a large role in reaching a catalogue's true potential. If we market through our city's local Twitter feed or news feed, offering enticing tips or attractions, we may find that we become a destination spot. For example, if your town is hosting a festival, often a popular local Twitter source will be tweeting events and news of interest. If the library can market through this Twitter source, followers may be introduced to remote services or online interactive catalogue opportunities that are related to the festival. This, in turn, may get tweeted by many other users, created numerous gateways into the community. While perhaps this isn't as easy as the example provided, it should provide all of us with a new way of thinking about marketing. It isn't about using our own resources but rather about tapping into popular resources that we may be unfamiliar with and that aren't controlled by our library. Have we tried to encourage our users to tweet about our newest catalogues? Have we held competitions regarding who can provide the "best" reviews or even competitions among our staff to think of new ways to use next generation catalogues in their areas of service?

While we can implement next generation catalogues and have a mild degree of success, to truly realize the potential of social catalogues, we need to think of marketing our catalogues in new ways and through media we've never considered in the past. In the end, we need to capture our users' interest through clever marketing so that they market for us and provide gateways into our online world.

NEW CATALOGUING STANDARDS

If you're a cataloguer, you've been involved in discussions regarding future cataloguing standards. The most talked about is Resource Description and Access (RDA). With RDA facing implementation in many libraries in the near future, there are ongoing discussions as to whether technology has surpassed the need for RDA implementation. RDA was "designed for the digital world and an expanding universe of metadata users" (RDA Tool-kit 2010). According to the founders of RDA, the benefits of RDA include the following:

- A structure based on the conceptual models of FRBR (functional requirements for bibliographic data) and FRAD (functional requirements for authority data) to help catalogue users find the information they need more easily
- A flexible framework for content description of digital resources that also serves the needs of libraries organizing traditional resources
- A better fit with emerging database technologies, enabling institutions to introduce efficiencies in data capture and storage retrievals (RDA Toolkit 2010)

While the debate for and against the implementation of RDA is an ongoing and controversial one, it will not be addressed here. However, there is a developing divide among academic libraries and public libraries about its implementation. While many public libraries view next generation catalogues as the key to dealing with an increasing amount of digital data and the means by which to gather and retrieve these data, academic libraries tend to favour RDA over next generation catalogues. Depending on whom you ask, professionals indicate that it is because the social catalogue is a better "fit" in the public environment, serving its specific patrons and their needs. Right or wrong, the true debate that might progress out of this divide is how to share data between academic and public libraries if one relies on traditional cataloguing methods and social catalogues while the other relies on a new standard for cataloguing. Will vendors then be forced to address back-end library catalogue concerns and forced to make our systems more robust in an attempt to share data, or will we see new consortiums for data sharing emerge, one with RDA users and one still using the existing, traditional cataloguing method?

THOUGHTS FROM PRACTICING PROFESSIONALS

It's easy to neatly place social catalogues and the features of social catalogues into yet another silo that stands alone from other library services. For every area of our profession, we're more familiar with the innovative ideas, developments, and changes happening within our area of expertise than we are with others. This is only natural. But in an environment where technology is blurring service lines and mutating into combined services that rely on each other more than ever before, it's important to understand what professionals throughout librarianship are saying about the changes we are facing.

As a cataloguer and librarian, next generation catalogues intrigue me, as does their potential for the future of librarianship, libraries, and core library services, cataloguing, and libraries in an online, mobile environment. However, it is also important to understand how other professionals view the changes to catalogues, what they see as challenges, the future directions of the catalogue, or the impact they will have on core library services.

Because we are discussing the future of next generation catalogues, two essays from practicing professionals can also offer some insight into possible directions we may want to take for the future of these catalogues as well as considerations that need to be made if they continue to grow in popularity and use. Brian Briscoe, the catalogue manager at St. Charles City-County Library District in St. Peters, Missouri, offers his opinion on what the future next generation catalogue may look like and how it will function. Dr. Louise Spiteri, academic program director, School of Information Management, Dalhousie University, Halifax, Nova Scotia, offers an examination of future issues we, as professionals, may face regarding the ethics of these catalogues and decisions or policies that may need to be created surrounding their use.

OPAIP: Online Public Access Information Portal
by Brian Briscoe

In considering the near future of library information access tools, I would like to introduce a new term: Online Public Access Information Portal. I hope it is a term that is adopted by the library world. It is a term use to describe the direction that I believe library information tools are heading and the way they must go in this time of rapid technological and social development.

The Online Public Access Information Portal is a software tool that allows our users to find all our information they wish, without harming our data, and while allowing the users to customize the information in any way that they desire.

The first consideration in any library change must be the end user. Changes to our information technology, cataloguing, and technical operations should be no different. Our users are becoming more technology savvy and more demanding of our resources than in the past. They are accustomed to Google-style key word searching with an easy-to-use interface. They use social networking not only to keep in touch with friends and business colleagues but also to gather, manipulate, and re-present information in ways that meet their needs. More information searching is being done remotely rather than inside the walls of our physical plants. So we must adjust to be most useful to our users.

There is much debate over what adjustments we should make. Libraries have a proud history of changing to meet the needs of our users, and this time will be no different. Despite several changes over time to our cataloguing rules, once again there are complaints that our catalogues are outdated and no longer useful. The biggest targets seem to be the machine-readable cataloguing (MARC) data format and our authority headings structure.

But the immediate abolishment of MARC would be a major error with negative repercussions that would last long into the future. While the gradual replacement of MARC with another catalogue data input standard is not beyond reason, the data that currently exist must be retained because of the high-quality data that are there. The data found in our MARC records contain more information in a more usable form than can be found in any other format currently available. A truly compatible format must be found and a data-loss-free transfer procedure developed before we can abandon these records.

Our authority file structure (also based on MARC) was developed over generations of library professionals for one purpose: to allow users to very specifically find the information they are seeking in our collections. It provides cross-referencing for users to input a single search term that collocates all resources that contain that subject, author, or title. It eliminates the need for users to sift through the thousands of unrelated hits that they receive when doing a key word search. Our authority files are the best information-narrowing tools available. They are not old and outdated; they are time proven.

So what can be done to make our information more accessible without abandoning MARC and authority structures? The vendor world is moving toward what it calls "discovery tools." These consist of software programs that reside on top of our catalogues, electronic databases, and other information resources to provide a single search interface for our users. They allow our users to simultaneously search our catalogues, our databases, and our websites using a usually single key word search box. They are user friendly and often provide links into the catalogue to allow for the searching of our catalogues using authority terms. They are a welcome development and a step in the right direction. A lack of unified resource searching and user-friendliness has plagued many libraries, and these discovery tools partially solve that problem.

But these discovery tools still have room for improvement. Because the format of our MARC catalogue data differs from that of our electronic databases and other resources, this may create uneven search results. Many of the discovery tools also either do not include a social networking aspect or do not integrate social networking effectively. So that aspect of customer service is lacking.

What our users seem to want is a tool that they can use to easily and effectively find information, manipulate the data to meet their needs, and share that information with friends, professors, and other networks. Discovery tools are meeting only a portion of the requirements.

What we need is a tool that meets all requirements. I propose an Online Public Access Information Portal. Envision a tool that uses much of the technology currently being used for the aforementioned discovery tools but that also takes the next step forward in meeting user needs while also, simultaneously, meeting the needs of libraries.

While allowing for continued searching across all library information sources, this tool would also recognize different data formats and allow for powerful searching within those resources using authority files to better target results.

Envision a tool that would facilitate user social networking while enabling users not only to easily find information as shown above but also to download, manipulate, and share that information with professors, friends, and other colleagues.

Moreover, this tool would maintain the security of the information sources so that copyright and security restrictions could be maintained by the owning or contracting library. This would require that the tool reside not within the data but outside the source.

Envision a library portal that allows users to easily and effectively find, gather, and manipulate the information they need while also protecting the information resources and data for the library. To do so would require a software program, much like the discovery tools noted earlier, that rests atop our catalogues and databases rather than within them. However, it requires a program with greater functionality and the social interaction capabilities mentioned above. This kind of solution allows for the gradual improvement and interoperability of MARC format and authority structures with other formats. It enables a smooth transition for users and library staff between new formats and technologies. And this solution does not require the near-term elimination of the integral practices of MARC and current authority structures.

An Online Public Access Information Portal creates a winning situation for everyone. Library cataloguers win because they can continue to be productive while gradually transitioning their records and other data to new systems. Users win because not only can they search easier and more efficiently, but they can also take advantage of new technologies to customize the information. And libraries win because they maintain control over their collections while reaping the benefits of happier users. The Online Public Access Information Portal would be a great asset to the future of libraries.

The Impact of Social Discovery Systems on Cataloguing Ethics by Louise Spiteri

INTRODUCTION

The library catalogue has long acted as an important and fundamental medium between users and their information needs. The traditional goals and objectives of the library catalogue are to enable users to search a library's collection to find items pertaining to specific titles, authors, or subjects. Today's library catalogues are competing against powerful alternatives for information discovery. Services offered by sites such as Amazon (http://www.amazon.com) and LibraryThing (http://www.librarything.com) allow members to interact with the catalogue and with each other by creating and participating in discussion groups; tagging or classifying items of interest in language that reflects their needs; sharing reading, listening, or viewing interests; and providing recommendations and ratings for selected items. These types of services serve to heighten library users' expectations of a library catalogue.

In the past few years, library discovery systems, such as AquaBrowser (http://www.medialab.nl), BiblioCommons (http://www.bibliocommons.com), and Encore (http://encoreforlibraries.com), have made important strides in providing an enhanced search and discovery experience for the users. These discovery systems have social-type Web 2.0 features that allow users to enhance the content of bibliographic records by adding their own tags, ratings, and reviews. These new social discovery systems can play an important role in helping information professionals meet one of the primary underlying principles of cataloguing, namely, that catalogue records be designed with the user in mind (IFLA 2009) and that, whenever possible, the needs of clients must be placed above other concerns (Koehler and Pemberton 2000).

The Principle of User Convenience

The information professions take pride in their client-oriented approach. Koehler and Pemberton (2000) examined the codes of ethics of 37 associations of information professions; while contents of these codes varied, what they agree that a primary duty of information professionals is to respond to the information and other related needs of the patron or client. Focussing on users and meeting their needs is an important ethical principle of cataloguing. Intner suggests that the goal of libraries is to serve their patrons and that Cutter's objects of the catalogue embody the aims of cataloguing, namely, that "cataloging operations should produce data that identify individual items and collocate related items" (Intner 2003, 72). Cutter instructed cataloguers to put the convenience of the public before their own needs.

Because access to and use of information is becoming increasingly important to the economic development of countries and of individuals, it is necessary to examine how culture influences information need, use, and behaviour (Steinwachs 1999) and, by extension, the design of catalogue records. In her discussion of the ethical imperatives for knowledge organization and representation, Beghtol (2002, 2005) refers to the concept of *cultural warrant*, which suggests that any knowledge organization or representational system should reflect the assumptions, values, and predispositions of the culture(s) in which it exists. Included in cultural warrant is the principle of *user warrant*, wherein individuals are considered to be members of a certain culture(s) and represent that culture(s) when they participate in the development and use of knowledge organization systems. Cultural warrant and hospitality provide important theoretical frameworks for the principle of user convenience.

While codes of ethics for information professionals may agree with the principle of user convenience, implementing this principle in practice is a far different matter: How can library catalogue records be designed to meet the potentially different cultural needs of their respective library communities? How do you reconcile these different needs with the desire to maintain the integrity of the content of catalogue records that follow standard procedures and guidelines? A further limitation to the creation of catalogue records that reflect user convenience is that it is often the case that not enough is actually known about user needs. Cataloguing rules and standards have not been developed with a sufficient understanding of user needs (Ferris 2008; Hufford 1992; Smiraglia 2009). With an insufficient understanding of user needs, cataloguers must often rely on their own judgment to customize catalogue records for user convenience. The process of customizing records is itself problematic since in the face of decreasing funding to cataloguing departments, library administrators often discourage cataloguers from this practice since it is often seen as a time-consuming and inefficient practice; it is cheaper, simpler, and faster to use purchased bibliographic vendors from vendors and cataloguing utilities with minimal modification (Hoffman 2009; Iliff 2004).

Social Discovery Systems, User Convenience, and Cultural Warrant

The main barriers to the creation of catalogue records that incorporate the principles of user convenience and cultural warrant can be summarized as follows:

1. Determining and reflecting the needs and cultural warrant of the users given that (a) the established lack of empirical knowledge of these needs, (b) the lack of interaction between the creators of the records and those who use them, and (c) that in pluralistic societies such as Canada, members of any given library community may represent a wide variety of cultures.
2. Maintaining the quality and integrity of the catalogue records given that (a) catalogue records need to fall within the structural framework of standardized cataloguing codes, (b) catalogue records often exist in a shared environment, and (c) catalogue departments may lack sufficient resources to create customized catalogue records.

The catalogue is a critical bridge between a library and members of its community: the catalogue record must provide information that clients would have obtained traditionally from browsing physically through an item and scanning its contents; this situation leads to the demand for fuller records with enhanced content, such as tables of contents, images, detailed summaries, and so forth. Creating enhanced content is a time-consuming and labour-intensive process. Social discovery systems may help address cataloguers' lack of (a) sufficient understanding of user convenience and cultural warrant and (b) time to customize records to accommodate these two principles. When users add metadata to existing catalogue records in the form of tags, ratings, or reviews, they are given the opportunity to express both their needs and their cultural points of view. Social discovery systems are a way to engage the library community with library staff since users can interact with bibliographic records and add their own metadata to reflect their needs and cultural warrant. Library staff can learn more about the members of the library community by examining tags, ratings and reviews, and create collections and services (such as readers' advisory) that more closely reflect the needs of the users. Social discovery systems can also enhance the role of the catalogue as a communication mechanism amongst the users themselves. User-assigned tags and reviews can help members of the library community connect with one another via shared interests and connections that may not be otherwise possible via the catalogue record that is created and controlled solely by the cataloguer. Social discovery systems can thus provide cataloguers with a way to interact, if indirectly, with users since cataloguers can observe user-created metadata.

One of the considerations for creating catalogue records in a Canadian environment is the cultural plurality that constitutes so many of its library communities. User-contributed metadata can assist in the expression of different cultural manifestations. Of course, the danger still exists that this metadata could reflect one culture above all others, particularly if that culture is predominant in a library community. To what extent will users from minority cultures feel free to contribute their own data? Will they be intimidated by the majority viewpoint? It would certainly be interesting to examine the extent to which user-contributed metadata do, in fact, reflect the cultural plurality of the communities served by the catalogue.

Social discovery systems may unnerve cataloguers who fear that user-contributed metadata could affect negatively the quality and integrity of catalogue records. In most social discovery systems, however, users can add metadata to a catalogue record but cannot interfere with existing contents. An important point to consider is that this record is created and controlled by library staff; the contents of this record cannot be changed or altered. The MARC record is closed to the public; users of the catalogue (other than authorized library staff) cannot, in fact, alter or modify the record. All that the end user can do is to *add* content to the MARC record in the form of tags, ratings, or reviews. The principles of user convenience and cultural warrant may, on occasion, require a degree of flexibility on the part of cataloguers in balancing the accurate content in the MARC record with user metadata that may be less accurate but still informative. Social discovery systems can allow catalogue records to balance the more controlled and formal nature of controlled vocabularies with the more fluid and grassroots language that reflects local users. User-contributed metadata could thus serve as an important way to examine to what extent controlled vocabularies reflect the needs of the user and to serve as an important mechanism by which to update these vocabularies.

Conclusion

Although placing clients above other concerns is the primary principle of most information professions, incorporating this principle into cataloguing practice is hampered by cataloguers' lack of knowledge of user needs; even if these needs were understood better, cataloguers often lack the time and resources to create catalogue records to meet these needs. Social discovery systems provide cataloguers with the opportunity not only to learn more about client needs but also to mitigate the time and cost needed to create customized catalogue records. User-contributed metadata in the form of tags, ratings, or reviews provide cataloguers with the opportunity to observe directly how users interact with catalogue records and adapt them to meet their needs. Social discovery tools can serve as a bridge between cataloguers' desire to create accurate catalogue records that conform to accepted cataloguing standards and their ethical imperative to ensure that these records meet the needs of the clients. User-contributed metadata provide clients with the opportunity to express their needs and cultural warrant and may thus serve also to increase users' interaction with each other and library staff via the catalogue. User-contributed metadata can be an invaluable resource by which to examine how people use and interact with catalogue records; furthermore, user tags can contribute to the examination and modification of controlled vocabularies such as

Library of Congress subject headings. The library catalogue has, until very recently, been controlled and hierarchical in structure, where information is imparted from library staff to the users: users have been the passive recipients and users of the library catalogue. As social discovery systems continue to be implemented across public and academic libraries in North America, it will be interesting to examine their impact on cataloguing practice and the extent to which they will encourage and facilitate the principle of user convenience.

FUTURE DEVELOPMENTS

Briscoe and Spiteri provide thoughtful discussion on the future of social catalogues and considerations that will have to be made. Throughout this book, a variety of perspectives on social catalogues have been explored. In many of the chapters, concrete examples have been provided that demonstrate how next generation catalogues, whether they are first generation or next next generation, can and will impact core library services.

In addition, the ever-increasing functionality of these catalogues reflects the changing nature of cataloguing and lead us to believe that there will be an impact on the skill set and knowledge demands for future cataloguers as well as frontline staff. These new catalogues and the changing nature of cataloguing also reflect the new and innovative ways we can offer core library services.

So what's in store for our next generation library catalogues? It's hard to predict what features will remain and what new features will be added to enhance these catalogues. While this book deals with what professionals can do now and the possibilities of what they can do in the near future, it's always interesting to take a glimpse at what other professionals are saying about the future of social catalogues and what they will become.

Many librarians ask, "So, I've implemented a social catalogue. Now what?" While there are many ideas and anecdotes provided throughout these chapters, there are also unanswered questions, including specific "how-tos" or simply "I've tried that and it didn't work." While some of these responses can be resolved by the results that future research will provide, additional results will stem from the discussions professionals are having about some of the outstanding issues that have yet to be resolved with library catalogues.

While discovery overlays, or interfaces, are the primary social catalogues that are being implemented in libraries, even fully integrated social catalogues that are part of the entire system have, up to this point, focussed only on patron needs. However, backroom staff as well as frontline staff often discuss the need for a social and collaborative "back end" to the library catalogue. Why can't the back end of the catalogue, where the majority of staff often access the system, be more intuitive, user friendly, and social? For example, many staff would love to use some of the faceted navigation features behind the scenes and be able to save these lists for future reference. This is often expressed by information desk and reference staff, where a need for mining the same data occurs frequently. Even the ability to run reports or lists would be made easier by more friendly interfaces on the back end of the catalogue or by the ability to tag existing reports or items for later use. For a cataloguer, it's more convenient to share local cataloguing and practice notes from within the software that is being used to catalogue than from storage on an outside platform or medium. Professionals, both frontline and backroom, can benefit greatly from future developments in this area. A robust back end to next generation catalogues would truly make it just that: a reinvention of the classic catalogue. Right now, many professionals are careful to remind us that what we call a social catalogue or next generation catalogue today is only a social online public access catalogue, or next generation online public access catalogue, and not a truly unique and innovative social catalogue as a whole.

While rethinking the entire back end of the catalogue will take time and likely many iterations before many professionals agree on what works and what doesn't, it also involves rethinking workflows in our Web-services environment. Issues to address if we move forward with a true "next generation catalogue" as a whole include how these back-end enhancements will deal with serials unpredictability, running reports, new materials in multiple formats, and data conversions when mining for information on the Web.

Other issues that have arisen in conversations among professionals are for both back-end enhancements of social catalogues as well as our online interface that are uniform but with different intentions. One interesting and innovative idea includes the ability to break apart data within our bibliographic records or, in other words, pulling and extracting data out of the catalogue for other purposes than just the traditional discover, find, and retrieve model. This can be as simple as trying to pull out how many editions and manifestations of one library's holdings on Jane Austen or extracting specific information out of back-end reports with the ability to manipulate those data into statistics.

What if there is no future for the integrated library system or library catalogue? In Chapter 4, the idea of a database taking the place of our existing library catalogues was introduced. Professionals are exploring alternatives to catalogues, considering the Internet or some other source as a replacement. Doesn't this really come down to what we define as a catalogue and its functions within the library? Does a library catalogue have to exist as part of an integrated library system for there to be a need for cataloguers? Will information no longer need to be organized and retrieved in a uniform and controlled environment? While the creators of this argument are found largely in the academic environment, they are just theories. But they are theories that should be acknowledged because it makes us all take time to thoughtfully consider what a library catalogue is and how it will function in the future. This book is providing ideas for its future and what it can become if we continue to push the limits of technology and invite innovative professionals to explore their ideas. Perhaps the largest force behind the future of library catalogues and their future will be the evidence we obtain through research conducted in academic circles and evidence-based practices in public libraries. Promoting discussion and theories for the future of the library catalogue is essential, but so is action. All of us are responsible for pushing the boundaries of our current services and advancing the technology we use to serve our users. Even in public libraries, encouraging staff to perform evaluations, hold focus groups, and engage users in discussions is vital to exploring what our next generation catalogues will be and where they will be housed.

CONCLUSION

The library catalogue is a social space and a community although, perhaps, not in the usual sense. While we're used to seeing tagging, reviews, and sharing on social media sites that invite individuals to cooperate in either a personal or a competitive sense, few collaborative spaces invite community groups or professionals to share their knowledge and expertise to create resource lists, provide leisure reading recommendations, or encourage learning, exploring, and discovering by interaction between professionals and community members. And, all the while, this space is a gathering space that promotes the role of our library in the community while giving the patrons a safe and welcoming place to interact to any degree that they wish—from "lurking" to contributing information that will shape the collections and programming within the library.

The ideas and materials presented throughout this book are meant to inspire professionals and to encourage them to think critically about how technology is impacting our core library services and to turn to the catalogue as an option for growing our presence outside of the library. It also acknowledges the real need to foster collaboration and respect between frontline and backroom staff in an age where our roles are not so specific but are, in many cases, now overlapping. Rather than promoting an environment of suspicion or concern over one professional's projects overlapping with another, social catalogues and their ability to enhance core library services should foster an environment of collaboration, sharing, and innovation among staff. While we may be concerned that cataloguers are walking too close to the readers' advisors job or a reference librarian is becoming too critical of our cataloguing practices, next generation catalogues and social technology in general are just that: social. Unfortunately, while we're busy trying to implement these sharing tools for our patrons, we aren't sharing our knowledge, skills, and expertise with each other. If we start looking for ways to collaborate, the library services we offer will benefit from it—as will our patrons.

While some of this book offers practical advice for the simple application of social tools into the catalogue and provides an alternate view of the importance of a library catalogue's role in the library over the website, it also offers a background in what the library catalogue can do and introduces technology and ideas that may be new to professionals. It is hoped that it has provided a critical and sometimes lighthearted or inspirational view of the future of the library catalogue and what our services can become if we view the catalogue as a social space and a community.

Targeted toward public library professionals, this book focusses on the emergence of next generation library catalogues and their increasing role in traditional library services. Exploring faceted navigation, user-generated content, and a variety of tools and applications being developed for these catalogues, it examines next generation library catalogues and their impact on remote library services and services offered within the physical walls of our libraries. Rethinking the traditional model of libraries, ideas for collaboration between technical services and frontline staff is presented.

While focussing on next generation catalogues, social software's impact on cataloguing practices, and the role of the cataloguer in public service, this book acts as a guide for all public library professionals. Rather than a cataloguing text, this resource takes advantage of and explores the possibilities of our strongest community and information tool: the library catalogue. However, written from a technical services perspective, it allows for a new point of view on traditional public library literature, often written by frontline professionals.

As a resource, this book also emphasizes the advantages of working together, presenting ideas and examples of public libraries using social tools within their catalogue or social catalogues that will explore the future of library services in an online, socially connected world. As a result, this book is a guide that shows that rather than lessening the importance of traditional library services, next generation catalogues will enhance them. In the end, it demonstrates that there is a future for our library catalogues and that it's an engaging, exciting, and collaborative one.

REFERENCES

Beghtol, Clare. "A Proposed Ethical Warrant for Global Knowledge Representation and Organization Systems." *Journal of Documentation* 58 (2002): 507–32.

Beghtol, Clare. "Ethical Decision-Making for Knowledge Representation and Organization Systems for Global Use." *Journal of the American Society for Information Science and Technology* 56 (2005): 903–12.

Connaway, Lynn Silipigni, Timothy J. Dickey, and Marie L. Radford. "'If It Is Too Inconvenient, I'm Not Going After It:' Convenience as a Critical Factor in Information-Seeking Behaviors." *Library and Information Science Research* 33 (2011): 179–90. doi:10.1016/j.lisr.2010.12.002.

Eklund, Amy. "Research on the Next Generation Catalog." Paper presented at the annual meeting for the American Library Association, Washington, D.C., June 2010. Available online at http://facstaff.gpc.edu/~aeklund (accessed November 12, 2010).

Ferris, Anna M. "The Ethics and Integrity of Cataloging." *Journal of Library Administration* 47 (2008): 173–90.

Hoffman, Gretchen L. "Meeting Users' Needs in Cataloging: What Is the Right Thing to Do? *Cataloging and Classification Quarterly* 47 (2009): 632–41.

Hufford, Jon R. "The Pragmatic Basis of Catalog Codes: Has the User Been Ignored?" (1992). Available online at http://esr.lib.ttu.edu/handle/2346/510 (accessed March 4, 2010).

IFLA. "Statement of International Cataloguing Principles." (2009). Available online at http://www.ifla.org/files/cataloguing/icp/icp_2009-en.pdf (accessed May 20, 2010).

Iliff, Julie M. "Cataloging: It's All about Connecting People with Information." *PNLA Quarterly* 68 (2004): 15.

Intner, Sheila S. "Struggling toward Retrieval: Alternatives to Standard Operating Procedures Can Help Librarians and the Public. *Cataloging and Classification Quarterly* 36 (2003): 71–86.

Jansen, B., A. Spink, and I. Taksa. "Research and Methodological Foundations of Transaction Log Analysis." In *Handbook of Research on Web Log Analysis.* Hershey, PA: Idea Group Inc. (IGI Global), 2009, 1–16.

Koehler, Wallace C., and J. Michael Pemberton. "A Search for Core Values: Towards a Model Code of Ethics for Information Professionals." *Journal of Information Ethics* 9 (2000): 26–54.

RDA Toolkit. Available online at http://www.rdatoolkit.org/home (accessed December 12, 2010).

Smiraglia, Richard P. "Bibliocentrism, Cultural Warrant, and the Ethics of Resource Description: A Case Study." *Cataloging and Classification Quarterly* 47 (2009): 671–86.

Steinwachs, Katarina. "Information and Culture—The Impact of National Culture on Information Processes." *Journal of Information Science* 25 (1999): 193–204.

BIBLIOGRAPHY

American Library Association. *The State of America's Libraries*. Chicago: American Library Association, 2009.

Beghtol, Clare. "A Proposed Ethical Warrant for Global Knowledge Representation and Organization Systems." *Journal of Documentation* 58 (2002): 507–32.

Beghtol, Clare. "Ethical Decision-Making for Knowledge Representation and Organization Systems for Global Use." *Journal of the American Society for Information Science and Technology* 56 (2005): 903–12.

"Beta: Read-Alike Recommendations." *LibraryThing Blog*. (March 1, 2010). Available online at http://www.librarything.com/blogs/librarything/2010/03/beta -read-alike-recommendations (accessed June 25, 2011).

Breeding, Marshall. "Next-Generation Library Catalogs." *Library Technology Reports: Expert Guides to Library Systems and Services* 43, no. 4 (2007).

Breeding, Marshall. "The State of the Art in Library Discovery 2010." *Information Today*, January/February 2010, 31–34.

Calhoun, Karen. "The Changing Nature of the Catalog and Its Integration with Other Discovery Tools." Final Report. *Library of Congress*. (March 2006). Available online at http://www.loc.gov/catdir/calhoun-report-final.pdf (accessed November 11, 2009).

Cohen, Steven M. "The Next Big 'Library Thing.'" *Library Journal* 45, no. 2 (2006): 33–35.

Connaway, Lynn Silipigni, Timothy J. Dickey, and Marie L. Radford. 2011. "'If It Is Too Inconvenient, I'm Not Going After It:' Convenience as a Critical Factor in Information-Seeking Behaviors." *Library and Information Science Research* 33: 179–90. doi:10.1016/j.lisr.2010.12.002.

Coyle, Karen. "The Library Catalog in a 2.0 World." Preprint. Published in *Journal of Academic Librarianship* 33, no. 2 (2009). Available online at http://www.kcoyle.net/jal_33_2.html (accessed November 29, 2009).

Dempsey, Lorcan. "Lifting Out the Catalog Discovery Experience." *Lorcan Dempsey's Weblog: On Libraries, Services and Networks.* (2006). Available online at http://orweblog.oclc.org/archives/001021.html (accessed November 11, 2009).

Eden, Brad. "Information Organization Futures for Libraries: Reinventing the OPAC." Chapter 3. *Library Technology Reports: Expert Guides to Library Systems and Services* 43, no. 6 (2007): 13–40.

Eklund, Amy. "Research on the Next Generation Catalog." Paper presented at the annual meeting for the American Library Association, Washington, D.C., June 2010. Available online at http://facstaff.gpc.edu/~aeklund (accessed November 12, 2010).

Emanuel, Jenny. "Next Generation Catalogs: What Do They Do and Why Should We Care?" *Reference and Users Services Quarterly* 49, no. 2 (2010): 117–20.

Ferris, Anna M. "The Ethics and Integrity of Cataloging." *Journal of Library Administration* 47 (2008): 173–90.

Griffis, Patrick, and Cyrus Ford. "Enhancing OPAC Records for Discovery." *Information Technology and Libraries*, December 2009, 191–93.

Hendrix, Jennifer C. "Checking Out the Future: Perspectives from the Library Community on Information Technology and 21st Century Libraries. *American Library Association.* Policy Brief no. 2 (2010).

Hildreth, Charles R. "Online Catalog Design Models: Are We Moving in the Right Direction?" Report submitted to the Council on Library Resources. (1995). Available online at http://myweb.cwpost.liu.edu/childret/clr-opac.html (accessed July 2, 2011).

Hoffman, Gretchen L. "Meeting Users' Needs in Cataloging: What Is the Right Thing to Do?" *Cataloging and Classification Quarterly* 47 (2009): 631–41 (accessed August 20, 2009) doi:10.1080/01639370903111999.

Hollands, Neil. "Improving the Model for Interactive Readers' Advisory Services. *Reference and User Services Quarterly.* Accessmylibrary. (March 22, 2008). Available online at http://www.accessmylibrary.com/coms2/summary_0286 -15531994_ITM (accessed December 12, 2010).

Hufford, Jon R. "The Pragmatic Basis of Catalog Codes: Has the User Been Ignored?" Available online at http://esr.lib.ttu.edu/handle/2346/510 (accessed March 4, 2010).

IFLA. "Statement of International Cataloguing Principles." Available online at http://www.ifla.org/files/cataloguing/icp/icp_2009-en.pdf (accessed May 20, 2010).

Iliff, Julie M. "Cataloging: It's All about Connecting People with Information." *PNLA Quarterly* 68 (2004): 15.

Intner, Sheila S. "Struggling toward Retrieval: Alternatives to Standard Operating Procedures Can Help Librarians and the Public. *Cataloging and Classification Quarterly* 36 (2003): 71–86.

Jansen, B., A. Spink, and I. Taksa. "Research and Methodological Foundations of Transaction Log Analysis." *Handbook of Research on Web Log Analysis.* Hershey, PA: Idea Group Inc. (IGI Global), 2009), 1–16.

Koehler, Wallace C., and J. Michael Pemberton. "A Search for Core Values: Towards a Model Code of Ethics for Information Professionals." *Journal of Information Ethics* 9 (2000): 26–54.

"Library Catalogs and Other Tools." *Oregon Library Association Quarterly* 15, no. 1 (2009). Available online at http://data.memberclicks.com/site/ola/olaq_15no1.pdf (accessed January 5, 2011).

Majors, Rice. "Local Tagging for Local Collections." *Computers in Libraries*, October 2009, 11.

Mangold, Amy. "Evansville Vanderburgh Public Library and NextReads/NoveList: Partners in Public Service." Paper presented at the American Library Association annual conference, Washington, D.C., June 27, 2010.

Markey, Karen. "The Online Library Catalog: Paradise Lost and Paradise Regained?" *D-Lib Magazine* 13, no. 1/2 (January/February 2007). Available online at http://www.dlib.org/dlib/january07/markey/01markey.html (accessed July 2, 2011).

May, Anne K., et al. "A Look at Readers' Advisory Services." *Library Journal* 125 (September 15, 2000): 40–44.

Mercum, Tanja, and Maja Zumer. "New Generation of Catalogues for the New Generation of Users: A Comparison of Six Library Catalogues." *Electronic Library and Information Systems* 42, no. 3 (2008): 243–61.

Mi, Jia, and Cathy Weng. "Revitalizing the Library OPAC: Interface, Searching, and Display Challenges." *Information Technology and Libraries*, March 2008, 5–22.

"New Recommendations: What Should You Borrow?" *LibraryThing Blog.* (June 22, 2011). Available online at http://www.librarything.com/blogs/librarything/2011/06/new-recommendations-what-should-you-borrow (accessed June 25, 2011).

"Nice Step toward What a Catalog Can Become." *AUTOCAT.* (June 2011). Available online at http://comments.gmane.org/gmane.education.libraries.autocat/40016 (accessed June 29, 2011).

Online Computer Library Center. *From Awareness to Funding: A Study of Library Support in America.* Dublin, OH: Online Computer Library Center, 2008.

Online Computer Library Center. *Online Catalogs: What Users and Librarians Want.* Dublin, OH: Online Computer Library Center, 2009.

Rainie, Lee. "Networked Creators: How Users of Social Media Have Changed the Ecology of Information." Paper presented at VALA Libraries Conference, Melbourne Australia, 2010. Available online at http://www.vala.org.au/vala2010/papers2010/VALA2010_Keynote_Rainie_Final.pdf (accessed July 2, 2011).

RDA Toolkit. Available online at http://www.rdatoolkit.org/home (accessed December 12, 2010).

Ross, Catherine Sheldrick, et al. "Summary of RA Library Visits: 2002–2010 (forthcoming).

Shearer, Kenneth D. "Readers' Advisory Transaction in Adult Reading." In *Guiding the Reader to the Next Book.* New York: Neal-Schuman, 1996, 17.

"Six Million More Seniors Using the Web Than Five Years Ago." *Nielson Wire.* (December 10, 2009). Available online at http://blog.nielsen.com/nielsenwire/online_mobile/six-million-more-seniors-using-the-web-than-five-years-ago (accessed December 12, 2010).

Smiraglia, Richard P. "Bibliocentrism, Cultural Warrant, and the Ethics of Resource Description: A Case Study." *Cataloging and Classification Quarterly* 47 (2009): 671–86.

Smith, Duncan. "Delivering RA Services to Readers in a Digital Age." *Ebooks: Libraries at the Tipping Point* (Library Journal Webcast, September 29, 2010).

Spiteri, L. F. "The Use of Collaborative Tagging in Public Library Catalogues." *Proceedings of the American Society for Information Science and Technology* 43 (2006): 1–5.

Spiteri, L. F. "Structure and Form of Folksonomy Tags: The Road to the Public Library Catalogue." *Webology* 4, no. 3 (2007). Available online at http://www.webology.org/2007/v4n2/a41.html (accessed June 20, 2011).

Spiteri, L. F., and Laurel Tarulli. *The Public Library Catalogue as a Social Space: Usability Studies of User Interaction with Social Discovery Systems.* Dublin, OH: Online Computer Library Center, 2011.

Steinwachs, Katarina. "Information and Culture—The Impact of National Culture on Information Processes." *Journal of Information Science* 25 (1999): 193–204.

Tarulli, Laurel. "A Budding Relationship: Romance between Readers' Services and the Catalogue." *Libraries Unlimited.* (2009). Available online at http://www.readersadvisoronline.com/ranews/jun2009/tarulli.html (accessed July 2, 2011).

Vielmetti, Edward. "Mobile Delivery: Focus on the Interface." *Netconnect*, Fall 2008, 6–8. Available online at https://wiki.ucop.edu/download/attachments/34668692/Focus+on+the+Interface.pdf?version=1&modificationDate=1275607597000 (accessed July 2, 2011).

Webb, Paula L., and Muriel D. Nero. "OPACs in the Clouds." *Information Today*, October 2009, 18–22.

Wyatt, Neal. "2.0 for Readers." *Library Journal* 132 (2007): 18. Available online at http://www.libraryjournal.com/article/CA6495211.html (accessed December 12, 2010).

Wyatt, Neal. "The Ideal Tool." *Library Journal* 134 (2009): 39–43.

Yu, Holly, and Margo Young. "The Impact of Web Search Engines on Subject Searching in OPAC." *Information Technology and Libraries*, December 2004, 168–80.

INDEX

About the Author

LAUREL TARULLI received her MLIS from the University of Alberta's School of Information Science in 2004. She is the 2009 recipient of the American Library Association's Esther J. Piercy Award and in 2010 received the Distinguished Alumni Award from her alma mater. Laurel and her research partner, Louise Spiteri, recently received an OLCL research grant to examine next generation catalogues. A consultant for NoveList and active member of her institution's readers' services team, Laurel holds the position of collection access librarian at Halifax Public Libraries in Halifax, Nova Scotia. Widely published, Tarulli is also the author of the Cataloguing Librarian Blog and frequent speaker at conferences on the topic of readers' services and the library catalogue.